Friday, ...

...e. of Our Lord be

...bt by this time, you h...

...nily which has befallen

...u will be anxious to k...

...your children; it is all

...ill it be effaced from ...

...det of the desola...

...dress

"Neither the earthquake nor the fire could daunt them. They were called the 'steel frame.' The name derived from the fact that when the destruction and havoc had all been wrecked, there stood forth in the bare city only the twisted steel frames of buildings. They were an invitation to an heroic people to come and build a bigger and a better San Francisco."

—Sister Vincentine Lancaster
From: *Faith Aflame*, 1952

St. Vincent's School
Mission and Third Streets, South of Market

Steel frames were a common sight throughout the city after the earthquake and fire. They were often the only remains of once important buildings—remains of the old San Francisco. And, they were a call for people to build a new San Francisco—to become the steel frames for rebuilding. The Sisters saw themselves as the steel frame for their new school on Fifth and Clementina.

Steel Frames

Eyewitness Accounts
of the
1906 San Francisco Earthquake and Fire

A Commemorative Book by the Daughters of Charity

2005

Steel Frames
A Commemorative Book by the Daughters of Charity
Copyright © 2005
Daughters of Charity
Province of the West
Seton Provincialate
26000 Altamont Road
Los Altos Hills, California 94022

Library of Congress Cataloging-in-Publication Data
    Steel Frames / Eyewitness Accounts of the 1906 San Francisco
    Earthquake and Fire / Daughters of Charity
    Los Altos Hills, CA ; Daughters of Charity, Province of the West
    (History - Daughters of Charity)
    152 p, 28.5 cm
    ISBN 0 - 9776643 - 0 - 9
1. Daughters of Charity — California — History — Religion
I. Daughters of Charity, Province of the West

Printed and bound in the United States by Año Nuevo Island Press.

Book Cover:
Photograph of the charred ruins of St. Vincent's School, Mission and Third,
courtesy of the Archives of the Archdiocese of San Francisco.

Illustrations of Daughters of Charity fleeing the burning city, South of Market,
by Sister Estela Morales, D.C.

Cover and jacket design by Marianne Hinckle, Año Nuevo Island Press.

In Loving Memory

of

all those who lost their lives

in the

1906 San Francisco Earthquake and Fire

May They Rest in Peace!

Eyewitness Accounts

April 18, 1906

August 6, 1906

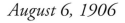

On Wednesday morning, April 18, 1906, a violent earthquake shook San Francisco and nearby cities. On this morning, the Daughters of Charity had nine Works in the cities affected by the earthquake.

Six Works were in San Francisco:
South of Market ~ two schools ~ demolished
Mission District ~ one hospital ~ demolished
Western Addition ~ one trade school ~ badly damaged
Silver Terrace ~ two orphanages ~ slightly damaged

Three Works were in nearby cities:
San Jose ~ one hospital ~ badly damaged
Hollister ~ one school ~ demolished
Santa Cruz ~ one orphanage/school ~ slightly damaged

All of these Works recovered from the disaster of April 18. No Work discontinued because of it, but three Works discontinued over the next decades. Six Works are still in existence today, and four are Works of the Daughters of Charity.

Table of Contents

This seal was originally affixed to the letters of
St. Louise de Marillac, who with St. Vincent de Paul
founded the Daughters of Charity in Paris, France, in 1633.
The English translation reads: *The Charity of Jesus Crucified
Urges Us.* This has been the seal of the Company
since 1644 and is the motivation behind the mission.

From: *Genesis of the Company,* 1633–1968

Introduction

By April of 1906, the Daughters of Charity had nine Works (Missions) in Northern California, and all were flourishing. Six of the Missions were in San Francisco:

St. Vincent's School, Mission and Third Streets, South of Market
St. Patrick's Boys' School, Natoma and Fourth Streets, South of Market
Mary's Help Hospital, Guerrero and Brosnan Streets, Mission District
St. Francis Technical School, Gough and Geary Streets, Western Addition
Mount St. Joseph Infant Asylum, Silver Avenue and Q Street, Silver Terrace
Mount St. Joseph's, N Street and 19th Avenue, Silver Terrace

In addition to the six Missions in San Francisco, the Sisters had three other Missions in the nearby cities of San Jose, Hollister, and Santa Cruz:

O'Connor Sanitarium, Race and San Carlos Streets, San Jose
Sacred Heart School, Sixth and West Streets, Hollister
Holy Cross School and Orphanage, Emmet and School Streets, Santa Cruz

Those Missions in the area South of Market and the Mission District were demolished; and although not demolished, the Mission in the Western Addition was severely damaged. The Missions in Silver Terrace were only slightly damaged and became places of refuge for the Sisters from South of Market and the Western Addition, as well as for others who needed food, clothing and shelter. Beyond San Francisco, the Mission in San Jose was severely damaged and the Mission in Hollister was demolished. The Mission in Santa Cruz, however, was only slightly damaged.

The Sisters living on all of these Missions wanted to keep the Sisters in Emmitsburg, Maryland (Central Administration), informed as to what was happening in San Francisco and the nearby cities. They sent telegrams as soon as possible and then began writing letters. From the Sisters' eyewitness accounts, we have come to know their story during the 1906 San Francisco Earthquake and Fire.

We want to share their story and have decided to let them tell it themselves in their own words through their writings. Their story unfolds through two phases:

The days of the earthquake and fire and immediate relief;
The weeks and months of recovery and rebuilding.

Their story is told primarily through letters written to Emmitsburg by Sisters Mary Joseph O'Leary, Vincentia Halligan, Louise McCarron, Mary Alice Maginnis, Eugenia Garvey, Genevieve Johnson, Victorine Fitzgerald, Teresa Hill, Helena McGhan and Martina Moran. The Sisters' writings have been edited for spelling/grammar/punctuation/paragraphing and adapted for clarity/readability, as well as, in a few instances, for anonymity/confidentiality.

We hope you will appreciate this story of the Daughters of Charity and will come to know and love the wonderful women who lived through the earthquake and fire and stayed to rebuild their Works amid the ruins and debris.

Chapter One

Turn of the Century

1900~1906

Nine Missions

San Francisco ~ San Jose ~ Hollister ~ Santa Cruz

*At the turn of the century,
the future looked promising for all the
Works of the Daughters of Charity
in San Francisco and the nearby cities.
The orphanages, the schools and the hospital
were all prospering, and a new hospital
was under construction.*

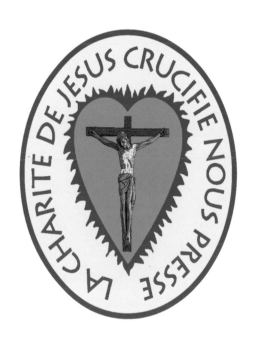

Early Years in San Francisco

*O*ur story of the Daughters of Charity in San Francisco began when five Sisters arrived from Emmitsburg, Maryland, in 1852 and established an orphanage and school on Market Street (near Montgomery). The orphanage was known as the Roman Catholic Orphan Asylum and the school as St. Vincent's School.

By the 1860s, the neighborhood of Market and Montgomery had become the business area of San Francisco and was no longer a suitable location for an orphanage. The Sisters purchased property about three miles away in a place then known as South San Francisco, in the Silver Terrace area. Here they built an orphanage for their infants and very young children and named it Mount St. Joseph Infant Asylum. Later, they moved their orphanage for older children from Market and Montgomery onto this same property in Silver Terrace and renamed it Mount St. Joseph's. On Mission Street, a few blocks from the original lot on Market and Montgomery, they built a new St. Vincent's School for their day pupils. By the 1870s, the orphanage and school, after so many years of close proximity, were separated by a distance of about three miles. The orphanages were located on the same property in Silver Terrace and the school in the area South of Market.

During the 1880s, the Sisters at Mount St. Joseph's opened a "trade school" for their older girls. The school was named St. Francis Technical School located on Gough and Geary Streets in San Francisco, Western Addition. Also, the Sisters at St. Vincent's School staffed a new school for boys. This school was called St. Patrick's Boys' School, located on Natoma Street just a few blocks from St. Vincent's (a girls' school). By the early 1900s, the Sisters were planning for their first hospital in San Francisco, Mary's Help, on Guerrero Street in the Mission District.

Earlier in the 1860s, the Sisters had opened Holy Cross School, an orphanage and school in Santa Cruz. Later in the 1880s and 1890s, they also opened Works in other nearby cities. In San Jose, they opened O'Connor Sanitarium, a hospital and home for the elderly, and in Hollister, Sacred Heart School for day scholars and boarders.

At the turn of the century, the future looked promising for all these Works. The orphanages in Silver Terrace as well as the trade school in San Francisco were all thriving. Also, the girls' school and boys' school in San Francisco were thriving. Mary's Help Hospital was under construction. The hospital and home in San Jose were prospering, and likewise the schools and orphanage in Hollister and Santa Cruz.

By April of 1906, the Daughters of Charity had nine Missions in northern California. Six were in San Francisco, in the South of Market, Mission District, Western Addition and Silver Terrace areas. Three were in the nearby cities of San Jose, Hollister and Santa Cruz.

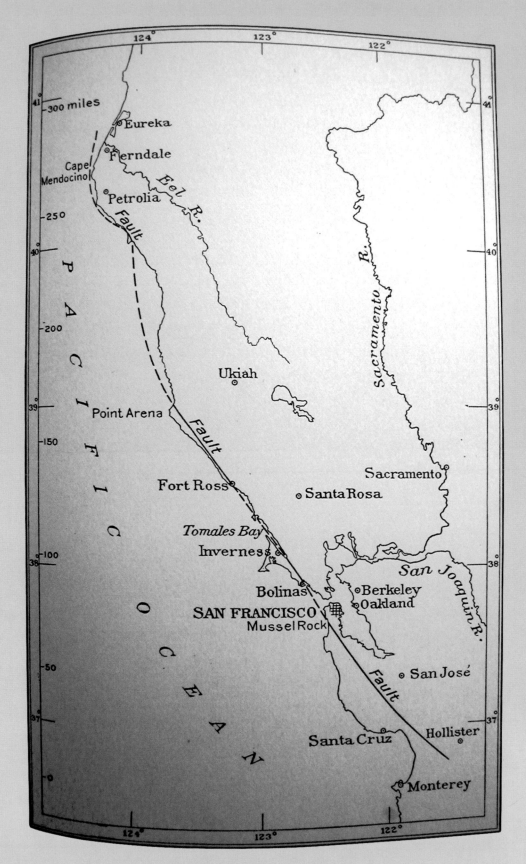

NORTHERN CALIFORNIA
San Andreas Fault, April 18, 1906

San Francisco

ST. VINCENT'S SCHOOL
Mission and Third Streets, South of Market

ST. PATRICK'S BOYS' SCHOOL
Natoma and Fourth Streets, South of Market

MARY'S HELP HOSPITAL
Guerrero and Brosnan Streets, Mission District

ST. FRANCIS TECHNICAL SCHOOL
Gough and Geary Streets, Western Addition

San Francisco

MOUNT ST. JOSEPH INFANT ASYLUM
Silver Avenue and Q Street, Silver Terrace

MOUNT ST. JOSEPH'S
N Street and 19th Avenue, Silver Terrace

San Jose

O'Connor Sanitarium
Race and San Carlos Streets

Hollister

Sacred Heart School
Sixth and West Streets

Santa Cruz

Holy Cross School and Orphanage
Emmet and School Streets

Chapter Two

Earthquake and Fire
April of 1906

Eyewitness Accounts
Telegrams ~ Letters ~ Memoirs

At 5:12 A.M. on Wednesday, April 18, 1906,
there was a violent earthquake that shook
the city of San Francisco. This was followed by
a devastating fire that burned out of control
for four days and three nights.

April 18, 1906

*A*t 5:12 A.M. on Wednesday, April 18, 1906, there was an earthquake that violently shook the city of San Francisco. This was soon followed by a fire that burned out of control, as there was no water to fight the fire because water mains had been severed in the earthquake. A four-square-mile area of San Francisco was demolished by earthquake and fire.

The neighborhoods South of Market Street were within this four-square-mile area and among the first to burn. St. Vincent's School (and the adjacent Sisters' residence on Minna Street) as well as St. Patrick's Boys' School were in this area and were demolished. Since both were day schools, the pupils were still in their homes at 5:12 A.M. The Sisters, however, were in their residence at the time of the earthquake.

The Sisters left the city and walked to the orphanages in Silver Terrace, where the earthquake had done little damage. They stayed there, but went back into the city during the day to nurse the wounded. Eventually, they went to the O'Connor Sanitarium in San Jose.

The neighborhood of Guerrero and Brosnan Streets was also within this four-square-mile area. Construction on the new Mary's Help Hospital was almost completed when it too was demolished.

The Gough and Geary neighborhood was just outside this four-square-mile area. Although St. Francis Technical School was badly damaged by the earthquake, it was still standing and became a relief center. Many of the Sisters stayed to help with the relief effort, while others went with the children to the orphanages in Silver Terrace.

The Silver Terrace area of South San Francisco was a distance of about two miles from the four-square-mile area that was burned. Mount St. Joseph's and Mount St. Joseph Infant Asylum had but little damage, and they became a refuge for the Sisters and children from South of Market and the Western Addition.

Outside the city of San Francisco, the earthquake wrought havoc as far south as San Jose, Hollister and Santa Cruz. In San Jose, the Sanitarium was damaged to the point where the patients were taken outside on the grounds and housed in tents. The Sacred Heart School in Hollister was demolished, and the children who were living there (the boarders) were housed in temporary quarters. The Holy Cross School in Santa Cruz, however, had but little damage.

The Sisters living on these Missions kept the Sisters in Emmitsburg informed about the happenings in San Francisco and the nearby cities. They sent telegrams and wrote letters. From their eyewitness accounts, we know their story during the 1906 San Francisco Earthquake and Fire.

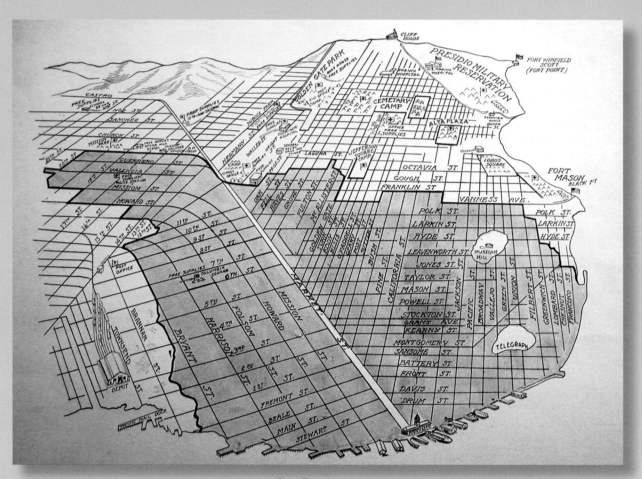

SAN FRANCISCO
Four Square Miles—Charred Ruins

ST. PATRICK'S CHURCH
Mission and Third Streets, South of Market

ST. VINCENT'S SCHOOL
Mission and Third Streets, South of Market

MARY'S HELP HOSPITAL
Guerrero and Brosnan Streets, Mission District

California

Telegrams

written by the Sisters
from the Missions
throughout California

San Francisco in Ruins

In the book *Denial of Disaster,* Gladys Hansen writes about the devastation of the city of San Francisco after the earthquake and fire of 1906. She indicates that this level of devastation would not be equaled until August of 1945, when the atomic bomb was dropped on Hiroshima.

SOURCE: *Denial of Disaster* by Gladys Hansen and others; published by Cameron and Company, San Francisco, 1989; page 107.

Word to Mother Margaret O'Keefe
in Emmitsburg

DAUGHTERS OF CHARITY, PROVINCE OF THE UNITED STATES
Emmitsburg, Maryland

SACRED HEART SCHOOL, HOLLISTER

Form No. 501.

THE WESTERN UNION TELEGRAPH COMPANY, OF BALTIMORE CITY.
CABLE SERVICE TO ALL THE WORLD.

This Company TRANSMITS and DELIVERS messages only on conditions limiting its liability, which have been assented to by the sender of the following message. Errors can be guarded against only by repeating a message back to the sending station for comparison, and the Company will not hold itself liable for errors or delays in transmission or delivery of Unrepeated Messages, beyond the amount of tolls paid thereon, nor in any case where the claim is not presented in writing within sixty days after the message is filed with the Company for transmission.
This is an UNREPEATED MESSAGE, and is delivered by request of the sender, under the conditions named above.

NUMBER	SENT BY	REC'D BY		CHECK
11	R Y	76	18 Paid	

RECEIVED at 945 P. m.   April 19th 1906

Dated Los Angeles Cal

To Mother Margaret —

Can get no word from Sisters in San Francisco
Am trying

Sister Mary Ann

SISTERS' HOSPITAL, LOS ANGELES

Form No. 501.

THE WESTERN UNION TELEGRAPH COMPANY, OF BALTIMORE CITY.
CABLE SERVICE TO ALL THE WORLD.

This Company TRANSMITS and DELIVERS messages only on conditions limiting its liability, which have been assented to by the sender of the following message. Errors can be guarded against only by repeating a message back to the sending station for comparison, and the Company will not hold itself liable for errors or delays in transmission or delivery of Unrepeated Messages, beyond the amount of tolls paid thereon, nor in any case where the claim is not presented in writing within sixty days after the message is filed with the Company for transmission.
This is an UNREPEATED MESSAGE, and is delivered by request of the sender, under the conditions named above.

NUMBER	SENT BY	REC'D BY		CHECK
3	64	M	8 Paid	

RECEIVED at 650 A. m.   April 20th 1906

Dated San Francisco Cal

To Mother Margaret

Miraculously escaped nursing wounded
well but everything burned

Sister Eugenia Garvey

ST. VINCENT'S SCHOOL, SAN FRANCISCO

Form No. 501.

THE WESTERN UNION TELEGRAPH COMPANY, OF BALTIMORE CITY
CABLE SERVICE TO ALL THE WORLD.

This Company TRANSMITS and DELIVERS messages only on conditions limiting its liability, which have been assented to by the sender of the following message. Errors can be guarded against only by repeating a message back to the sending station for comparison, and the Company will not hold itself liable for errors or delays in transmission or delivery of Unrepeated Messages, beyond the amount of tolls paid thereon, nor in any case where the claim is not presented in writing within sixty days after the message is filed with the Company for transmission.
This is an UNREPEATED MESSAGE, and is delivered by request of the sender, under the conditions named above.

NUMBER	SENT BY	REC'D BY		CHECK
	64	H	16 Paid	

RECEIVED at 730 A. m.   April 20th 1906

Dated Los Angeles Cal

To Mother Margaret

Hollister Mission Street probably technical
destroyed all Sisters safe. Father Glass
gone up to assist Sisters

Sister Mary Ann

SISTERS' HOSPITAL, LOS ANGELES

THE WESTERN UNION TELEGRAPH COMPANY, OF BALTIMORE CITY

CABLE SERVICE TO THE WORLD.

This Company TRANSMITS and DELIVERS messages only on conditions limiting its liability, which have been assented to by the sender of the following message. Errors can be guarded against only by repeating a message back to the sending station for comparison, and the Company will not hold itself liable for errors or delays in transmission or delivery of Unrepeated Messages, beyond the amount of tolls paid thereon, nor in any case where the claim is not presented in writing within sixty days after the message is filed with the Company for transmission. This is an UNREPEATED MESSAGE, and is delivered by request of the sender, under the conditions named above.

NUMBER 4 — SENT BY H — REC'D BY M — CHECK 10 Paid

RECEIVED at 930 A.M. — April 20th 1906

Dated San Jose Cal

To Mother Margaret—

Buildings damaged no loss of life absolutely no one injured

Sister M Victorine

O'CONNOR SANITARIUM, SAN JOSE

THE WESTERN UNION TELEGRAPH COMPANY, OF BALTIMORE CITY

CABLE SERVICE TO ALL THE WORLD.

This Company TRANSMITS and DELIVERS messages only on conditions limiting its liability, which have been assented to by the sender of the following message. Errors can be guarded against only by repeating a message back to the sending station for comparison, and the Company will not hold itself liable for errors or delays in transmission or delivery of Unrepeated Messages, beyond the amount of tolls paid thereon, nor in any case where the claim is not presented in writing within sixty days after the message is filed with the Company for transmission. This is an UNREPEATED MESSAGE, and is delivered by request of the sender, under the conditions named above.

NUMBER 10 — SENT BY AB — REC'D BY H — CHECK 10 Paid

RECEIVED at 8 P.M. — April 28nd 1906

Dated Santa Cruz Cal.

To Mother Margaret—

Slightly damaged all well room for Sisters children if needed

Sister Helena McShau?

HOLY CROSS SCHOOL, SANTA CRUZ

THE WESTERN UNION TELEGRAPH COMPANY, OF BALTIMORE CITY

CABLE SERVICE TO ALL THE WORLD.

This Company TRANSMITS and DELIVERS messages only on conditions limiting its liability, which have been assented to by the sender of the following message. Errors can be guarded against only by repeating a message back to the sending station for comparison, and the Company will not hold itself liable for errors or delays in transmission or delivery of Unrepeated Messages, beyond the amount of tolls paid thereon, nor in any case where the claim is not presented in writing within sixty days after the message is filed with the Company for transmission. This is an UNREPEATED MESSAGE, and is delivered by request of the sender, under the conditions named above.

NUMBER 2 — SENT BY JO — REC'D BY M — CHECK 19 Collect—

RECEIVED at Emmittsburg Md 730 A.M. April 30th 1906

Dated San Francisco Calif April 24th

To Mother Margaret—

Earthquake baffles description fire under control Thank God Sisters and children of all our homes safe no one injured

Sister Mary Loins

MOUNT ST. JOSEPH INFANT ASYLUM, SAN FRANCISCO

San Francisco

Letters

written by the Sisters
from the Missions
in San Francisco

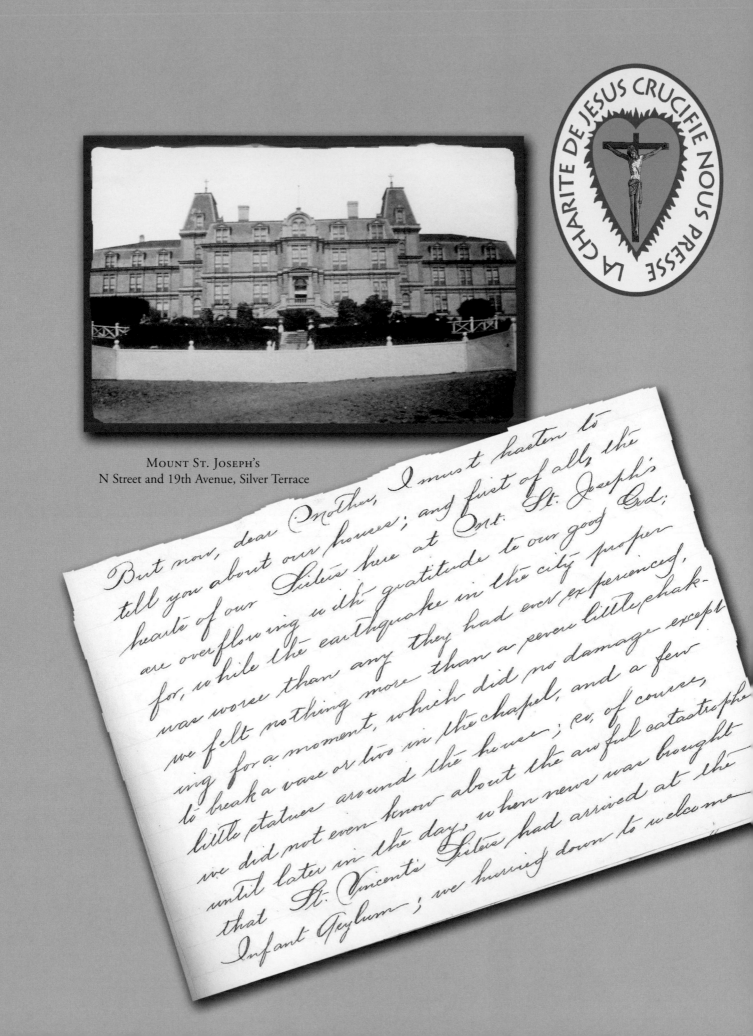

MOUNT ST. JOSEPH'S
N Street and 19th Avenue, Silver Terrace

But now, dear Mother, I must hasten to tell you about our houses; and first of all, the hearts of our Sisters here at Mt. St. Joseph's are overflowing with gratitude to our good God; for, while the earthquake in the city proper was worse than any they had ever experienced, we felt nothing more than a severe little shaking for a moment, which did no damage except to break a vase or two in the chapel, and a few little statues around the house; &, of course, we did not even know about the awful catastrophe until later in the day, when news was brought that St. Vincent's Sisters had arrived at the Infant Asylum; we hurried down to welcome

[Mount St. Joseph's]
San Francisco, California
April 20, 1906

My very dear Mother,

*T*he grace of Our Lord be with us forever!

No doubt by this time, you have learned of the awful calamity which has befallen our poor city, but I feel you will be anxious to hear a few details regarding your children. It is all so dreadful that never will it be effaced from our memory; although in the midst of the desolation and sorrow, we can feel the immense goodness of God and the truth of what St. Vincent says, "Our Lord watches over the Daughters of Charity with a most special care."

On Wednesday morning, April 18 at 5:15, a most fearful earthquake awoke the slumbering inhabitants. First, a low rumbling sound which in a moment grew louder and louder followed immediately by the crashing of falling buildings as they caved in, burying hundreds of poor victims beneath the ruins; while amid the frightful disorder could be heard the shrieks of the wounded and the moans of the dying. The streets were in an instant thronged with men, women and children, homeless and forlorn, having in that moment lost everything but their lives. The scenes were heart-rending, but the worst was still to come.

Directly after the earthquake, fire broke out which in the space of a few hours swept over the doomed city. The awful earthquake had burst the main pipes causing a great scarcity of water; so the firemen had simply to let the flames mount higher and higher, spreading with such rapidity that the panic-stricken people fled for their lives, leaving not only their homes to be demolished, but in many cases, their clothing, money; in fact, all they possessed.

As the fire was completely beyond control, the city authorities thought the best plan would be to blow up the tall brick buildings with dynamite in order to keep the flames in a certain district and prevent them from encircling the entire city. You may imagine our feelings, my very dear Mother, as almost every minute a loud report could be heard announcing the fall of some huge structure; while the columns of smoke which hung over us, darkened the sky and made one feel that the day of judgment had come at last. Several times throughout the day, the earth trembled so that many were afraid to remain indoors.

But now, dear Mother, I must hasten to tell you about our Houses. And first of all, the hearts of our Sisters here at Mount St. Joseph's are overflowing with gratitude to our good God; for while the earthquake in the city proper was worse than any they had ever experienced, we felt nothing more than a severe little shaking for a moment which did no damage except to break a vase or two in the Chapel and a few little statues around the house. So, of course, we did not even know about the awful catastrophe until later in the day when news was brought that St. Vincent's Sisters had arrived at the Infant Asylum. We hurried down to welcome them, fearing the worst which indeed proved true, as both house and schools had disappeared. But I shall not dwell on their sad experiences as doubtless you have heard before this from Sister Eugenia.

It is sufficient to say they were in a sorry plight; their terror of the early morning had not yet left them. They were all unnerved, sorrowful and weary, having walked nearly the entire distance. But no one could blame them for such feelings. Just picture them in their Chapel making meditation in perfect quiet, when all at once the statues began to fall with a tremendous crash; benches completely overturned; plaster fell in large pieces from walls and ceiling; sanctuary light extinguished; in fact, utter desolation. One of the Sisters says she ran as quickly as possible to the yard, but there a fearful sight met her gaze: bricks, plaster, wood, glass, all in confusion; while immediately opposite their gate on Minna Street a house had caved in and, horrible to relate, the occupants were in eternity.

They told us also that the Priests came over as soon as possible to see if they were all alive. They received general absolution and shortly after, Holy Communion. The Priest then said, "Sisters, flee for your lives; you have no time to lose." So, acting on this advice, they fled; though not moments too soon as the flames were directly at their back. Was it not sad, dear Mother, to be obliged to leave with scarcely any extra clothing, taking just what they had on? So, here they are at present, divided up between the two houses, we having the greater number as there is more room here. They went into the city yesterday and are also there today to help take care of the wounded. The scenes they describe would make your heart sick. May God pity these poor creatures!

Sister Louise is also here with her Sisters and girls. The Technical School was badly shaken up, but is still standing. The Sisters are as well as can be expected and all seem very, very grateful for the visible protection of Divine Providence. Yesterday and today, the sun has been shining brightly, making it nice and warm for the poor homeless people who are finding what shelter they can on the hillsides. A Relief Committee has been organized and they are doing good work, although it takes time to reach all. In the meantime, they are coming to our door, begging for bread; but the Captain of Police advised us not to give out the food we had, as our own family is large and provisions hard to obtain, especially bread. So you see, my very dear Mother, God has been pleased to chastise us, but with it all, He has shown such mercy and goodness to your Western daughters. We had a Mass of Thanksgiving in our Chapel this morning at which the children sang the Te Deum. I am sure all our hearts sang in unison with their innocent little voices. We shall have Forty Hours devotion on Sunday. So, you see we intend to keep on praying.

Dear Sister Stanislaus R. is really wonderful. Although very weak, she sits up part of the day and actually came down to Mass this morning. And now my very dear Mother, begging your prayers for us all and assuring you of my filial affection, I remain yours in the Sacred Heart,

Sister M. Joseph O'Leary, U.D.o.C.S.o.t.P.S.
[Unworthy Daughter of Charity
Servant of the Poor Sick]
[On Mission at Mount St. Joseph's,
Silver Terrace]

MOUNT ST. JOSEPH INFANT ASYLUM
Silver Avenue and Q Street,
Silver Terrace

2 destruction of buildings. Explosives
dynamite and other explosives
the terrible vibrations of which
filled all with real terror.
Our houses and grounds were
covered with ashes, cinders and
fragments of wood, so that we
were hourly in danger of igniting
but the earnest and fervent prayers
of our hundreds of little ones, proved
our safety and except a great fright
and some damaged chimneys
and cracked wall, with fallen
plaster, we escaped safe and
unharmed, while hundreds are
said to have been killed by
falling buildings, or suffocation
by smoke and fire. Our hearts are
most grateful for so striking a
protection to our hundred of helpless ones

Mount St. Joseph Infant Asylum
San Francisco, [California]
April 20, 1906

My very dear Mother

*T*he grace of Our Lord be with us forever!

Our dear Sister Mary has commissioned me to write you of our providential escape and safety from death and danger by a series of terrible earthquakes on Wednesday morning at 5:30 followed immediately by terrific fires in the business and most flourishing section of the city. The water supply was cut off entirely by the earthquake having severed the water conduits, so the firemen with all their most modern apparatus were powerless to stay the flames. So, recourse was had to the destruction of buildings by dynamite and other explosives, the terrible vibrations of which filled all with real terror. Our Houses and grounds were covered with ashes, cinders and fragments of wood, so that we were hourly in danger of igniting. But the earnest and fervent prayers of our hundreds of little ones proved our safety, and except a great fright and some damaged chimneys and cracked wall with fallen plaster, we escaped safe and unharmed; while hundreds are said to have been killed by falling buildings or suffocation by smoke and fire. Our hearts are most grateful for so striking a protection to our hundreds of helpless ones.

The ravages of the earthquake in some portions of the city are frightful. Entire blocks of buildings have sunk almost to the street level; wide openings are to be seen; sidewalks collapsed, with the buildings in many cases burying the inmates or severely injuring many. Women and children are now huddled together on sidewalks, vacant lots and the hillsides with all their saved belongings. Even the cemeteries were utilized as refuge, which some hours later had to be abandoned to escape the approaching flames. Nearly all the Catholic Churches are entirely destroyed either by fire or earthquakes, so that the affliction and sufferings of our poor people is simply frightful.

Some of us spent yesterday among the poor sufferers, who lost their all in home, etc., but are gratefully blessing and thanking God for preserving their lives while they are surrounded by dead and dying. The injured were placed in hospitals, both public and private, later hastily removed to halls, car houses and school houses, some of which collapsed burying the patients in the ruins. The scenes of sorrow and suffering we witnessed yesterday were heart-rending and we could only sympathize and try to comfort some, where all were destitute.

Appeals came every hour to our dear Sister Mary for food or shelter for entire families and never in vain. Our family is increased by the addition of forty boys from the Youth's Directory, now in ruins. Food and water are generously bestowed and never one refused, for God will provide even by a multiplication of loaves for His own dear children of our households. Our Sisters from St. Vincent's School, now homeless, are divided between our two [orphanages]. Also, the Sisters and girls from the Technical School are at the upper [orphanage] and all were accorded a most sincere and heartfelt welcome by our dear Sister Mary and Sister Stanislaus R.

All are now safe and secure from danger as the flames are now under control. And Relief Committees are being formed and assistance in money, food and supplies of all kinds are pouring in from all quarters of our eastern cities as well as those surrounding our afflicted city. Our Chapel sustained considerable damage to our Easter decorations, for our altar was totally bereft of vases, candelabras; and every movable article was found shattered on the floor by the long continued earthquake. But that we are not forced to mourn the loss or injury of even one of our dear little children makes our hearts overflow with gratitude and renders light and easy the inconveniences of these days of sorrow and distress in our afflicted city.

Our dear Sister Mary has stood her increased anxieties and cares since last Wednesday very well, for sleepless and anxious nights with doubly laborious days have been her share and they are not yet over. Our surrounding hillsides and vacant grounds are covered with refugees of men, women and children, with the remains of their household goods piled about them. [They are] living, cooking and sleeping in the open air and coming hourly to ask for water and food that is freely given. We fondly trust the worst is over if our dear Lord does not further chastise our sins by pestilence arising from broken sewers, lack of water and over-crowded quarters.

Begging prayers for our afflicted and suffering city and with assurances of affectionate greetings from dear Sister Mary and each of our Sisters as if named, I remain very affectionately,

Sister Vincentia Halligan, U.D.o.C.S.o.t.P.S.
[On Mission at Mount St. Joseph
Infant Asylum, Silver Terrace]

P.S. All communication by telegraph, telephone and mail has been cut off since Wednesday; else you would have heard from Sister Mary. A slight shock of earthquake accompanied the writing of this letter and caused me to drop my pen and repeat our heartfelt Aspiration, "Holy God, etc." Our dear Sister Frederica keeps up well amid our excitement and comforts and cheers by her prayers. *SV*

My dear Mother,

*T*he grace of Our Lord be with us forever!

I am sure your maternal heart must be greatly distressed and anxious to hear something about your California children. San Francisco seems to have been the victim and it may be that God's wrath is justly [irritated] against us. I am sure whatever you have heard or read about it has not been exaggerated. The scene was and is [still] something terrifying. Portions of the city are still burning though the principal parts are flattened to the ground. The Authorities removed the dead and dying to the Mechanics Building, but it was not long even that was consumed by fire with all the corpses. The dead were lying in the streets and hillsides; some they buried in the Plaza and others they threw into the Bay. The Fire Department was almost powerless as the earthquake had broken a great many of the main water pipes, thereby emptying the reservoirs.

April 23, 1906

This is the first opportunity I have had to finish my letter since writing the above. Since then the fire has carried everything before it with the exception of a few houses in our neighborhood. Among them is the Cathedral which was saved by three of the priests and a sailor climbing the spire and letting down a rope to which the people below attached a hose and for three hours they used it on the fire. [Also, among them are] the Madams of the Sacred Heart and our House, along with others for a block or so. If the Cathedral had gone, it would have taken everything with it. The Madams have turned their place into a hospital, and ours is used for the destitute and homeless men, women and children. Our House was badly shaken up from the earthquake; the roof was broken in from the fall of the chimney and one girl narrowly escaped; but thank God all got out without the least confusion. And most unfortunate for me, I sprained my ankle Easter Monday as we had taken the children across the Bay for the day and I slipped on the grass and crushed it pretty badly; but thank God I can get around with the aid of a chair.

We brought all our children out to Sister Stanislaus R.; but since our Sisters, all but Sister Rufina, are at the School I thought it best to be there too. Added to our misfortune, a pelting rain and wind arose last night that it seemed to me [all] would be blown off the earth entirely. It certainly will purify the city if the people will not be carried off by pneumonia. Pray for us, dear Mother, that we may be directed by God. I shall write you again in a few days.

Devotedly,

Sister Louise [*McCarron,* U.D.o.C.S.o.t.P.S. On Mission at St. Francis Technical School, Western Addition]

FATEFUL BUILDING

SAN FRANCISCO, April 18.—The scene at the Mechanics' pavilion during the early hours of the morning and up until noon, when all the injured and dead were removed, because of the threatened destruction of the building by fire, was one of indescribable sadness. Sisters, brothers, wives and sweethearts searched eagerly for some missing dear ones. Thousands of persons hurriedly went through the building inspecting the cots on which the sufferers lay in the hope that they would locate some loved one that was missing.

The dead were placed in one portion of the building, and the remainder was devoted to hospital purposes. After the fire forced the nurses in positions to desert the building, the eager crowds followed them to the Presidio and Children's Hospital, where they renewed their search for missing relatives.

THE CALL-CHRONICLE-EXAMINER
San Francisco, Thursday, April 19, 1906

41

Mission and Third Streets, South of Market

SISTER MARY ALICE MAGINNIS

In the book *Denial of Disaster,* Gladys Hansen writes about the fires that broke out in the area South of Market almost immediately after the earthquake: in the lodging houses and Prost's Bakery near Howard and Sixth; in the Saloon on the corner of Minna and Third; at the Gas and Electric Station at Jessie and Third. (These were the fires that surrounded St. Vincent's School, located at Mission and Third, and the adjacent Sisters' residence at Minna and Third: the lodging houses and Prost's Bakery fires were a few blocks to the south and west; the Gas and Electric Station fire was a couple blocks to the north; the Saloon fire was on the corner.)

SOURCE: *Denial of Disaster* by Gladys Hansen and others; published by Cameron and Company, San Francisco, 1989; pages 18–26, 61.

San Francisco, [California]
April 21, 1906

[Dear Mother Margaret,

*T*he grace of Our Lord be with us forever!]

I know you have received papers telling about the sad disaster to our city. The Catholic Churches and Schools have nearly all disappeared. St. Vincent's was first on the list of Schools, St. Patrick's Church first among the Churches. Could you ever have imagined that our beautiful, strong and well-built Church could go? The steeple fell across Mission Street and crushed the houses. Then, do you remember the great tower by the electric works on Jessie Street? That came down behind the Church. Even with all these earthquake terrors the loss of life and property would not have been so great, but fires started in different directions: behind us, on the sides and on the corners, and no water could be had, for the earthquake had wrenched the pipes. There lay the city at the mercy of the flames! We received our dear Lord in the parlor the morning we left and we were out before seven o'clock, running from the fire. May God be praised! We started down Mission Street from Second and could not get to Third by any means. No wagons were to be had and we just escaped with our lives.

We went to St. Mary's Hospital where we found the Sisters and patients in great excitement. They feared only the earthquake; how little thought they that the fire was coming upon them. They gave us a cup of coffee and the poor Sisters breakfasted with us. After breakfast we went into their Chapel and united with them in pleading for mercy; we then took the road for Mount St. Joseph's, where we arrived more dead than alive, but happy to find a shelter with our dear Sisters. When our Blessed Lord sees fit to use us again, we are here awaiting his decrees. I am glad that I was with the dear old place until it passed out of existence. I have since offered to His Infinite Goodness, many times, every good word we ever said there for His love and every act we performed.

Sister Mary Alice [*Maginnis,*
U.D.o.C.S.o.t.P.S.
On Mission at St. Vincent's School,
South of Market]

[Sister Mary Alice was the niece of Father John Maginnis, the first Pastor of St. Patrick's Church. She was a young girl of twelve when she came to San Francisco in 1854 and was among the earliest pupils at St. Vincent's School. She became a Daughter of Charity in 1861 and was missioned to her own St. Vincent's School, then on Jessie Street and later on Mission Street.]

After many slight shocks of earth quake we became tranquil & began to think of others. We were safe in either Foundling House or R.C.O. Asy. some Sisters were in both places, but I felt that the Sisters of Charity should be braver than that — Ro. Sr. Aloisi & I went down & begged a man to bring us to the city where masses of suffering creatures lay in big halls etc. He brought us to a car house where the dying lay thick upon the floor. The nurses were dropping on the floor from exhaustion Dr. was glad to see us so I sent back to San Francisco for 8 m

Sister Eugenia Garvey

[O'Connor Sanitarium]
San Jose, California
April 21, 1906

My own Beloved Mother,

*T*he grace of Our Lord be forever with us!

This is the first chance I have had of writing you as I am cramped in a tiny tent on the [O'Connor] Sanitarium lawn where all the sick are sheltered. No words can depict the awful horrors through which your daughters of St. Vincent's have just passed. On account of our position in the business part of the great city, the horrors of the fire followed the terrible earthquake. I will try to tell you just what we have passed [through].

Our dear Sisters were in the Chapel at 5:15 A.M. I had been very sick with sore throat and pleurisy and for three days under Doctor's care (Doctor feared pleural pneumonia). Sister and I slept on the fourth floor of the Mission Street School. After a night of pain I was sleeping soundly when the terrific rocking began. We dashed down the long corridors and steep stairways. The stairs were going from side to side, the walls falling in, the plaster and gas fixture falling all about us. We reached the ground floor unhurt.

The dear Sisters in the Chapel had the benches twisted from under them, the statues fell to the ground, and the Stations of the Cross turned faces to the wall. They rushed out and up the creaking stairway to find me (I was in the Mission Street building). When they reached the fourth floor they found me gone. I was calling them down to the front door. They all got down safe and sound, not a scratch on any Sister. I got habit on and with a blanket about me rushed out on the street with the rest of humanity.

When the rocking ceased, we returned to the ground floor. Our good Priests rushed over to see us. One gave us conditional absolution and he brought down the Blessed Sacrament and gave us Holy Communion. Then we felt happy. In less than ten minutes the firemen rushed in and told us to leave at once and seek safety. We wanted to get our good habits, books, etc.; but already our house was on fire, and a policeman and Father Horan, our good friend, led us through the surging mass of humanity. (On our sidewalk a crazed bull was goring a man to death; soon, however, the animal was killed.)

We reached St. Mary's Hospital, Sisters of Mercy; there we were received kindly, given good hot coffee and a piece of bread, but the Hospital was threatened with fire and we started off to South San Francisco. (Later on, the sailors of the big vessel, Manchuria, carried the patients and Sisters of Mercy to their vessel on the Bay where they are in safety.) Almost falling upon our faces, almost, we reached [the orphanages] about eleven o'clock and remained there that night. We sat up watching the flames consume our poor city. I never took my eyes off the flames the entire night. Even now when I close my eyes I see flames, nothing but flames.

After many slight shocks of earthquake, we became tranquil and began to think of others. We were safe in either [Mount St. Joseph Infant Asylum or Mount St. Joseph's], some Sisters were in both places. But I felt that the Sisters of Charity should be braver than that, so Sister Alexis and I went down and begged a man to bring us to the city, where masses of suffering creatures lay in big halls, etc. He brought us to a car house where the dying lay thick upon the floor. The nurses were dropping on the floor from exhaustion. Doctors were glad to see us, so I sent back to South San Francisco for eight more Sisters. All day we knelt beside the sufferers, washed their faces and hands, fixed their beds and pillows, attended to other wants and proved ourselves acceptable nurses. We cared for the sick whilst the nurses went off to get a little rest in the cars standing about us. We left in the evening, and at the same time the patients had to be moved for the second time to another place of safety. We got an old rag wagon to take us to South San Francisco, paying the driver $5.00 for the ride.

Next morning one of our good Priests said Mass for us at the Infant Asylum. After Mass, Sisters Alexis, DeSales, Joannes, Hyacinth, Estelle, Josephine, Caroline and Cecilia and I started to the city in a big wagon which we met on the street. We went to find the sick, but they had been taken on trains to San Mateo. Doctors told us to go there and trains were taking people out of the city free, so we took the train for San Mateo. We found the sick in a barn, but many nurses to look after them; so we went on to San Jose where we hoped to find the [O'Connor] Sanitarium intact, but to our astonishment the building was deserted and the sick were in tents on the grounds. Oh, Mother, here we received such a sisterly welcome. Our dear Sisters rushed with open arms to grasp us and bid us welcome, for they feared that we had been consumed in the flames.

Although I am stiff from the walking and bending all day over the sick that were laid on the floor of the car house, I am, considering all things, pretty well. Our Sisters are working with the nurses and all the Sisters. If the sun comes out, I'll feel well and I can work well with the sick and I am in my glory doing it. Our dear Sisters are heartbroken, fearing that never again will we be together with our hundreds of dear children in poor old St. Vincent's. I comfort them by telling them that our dear Superiors will not separate us after all we have passed through together, that as soon as possible we will have a temporary school and the poor children will throng to us.

Archbishop Montgomery must be in a dreadful state; churches, convents and big schools are no more. There is nothing left of St. Patrick's Parish, Church, Schools, Priests' new house, all gone!! All the Churches in southern part of the city are gone. The city is under martial law; the soldiers are shooting down any men who are found taking things. As we drove along the streets yesterday, there was the sight of the agonizing faces of the people who stood meekly in long lines awaiting their turn to get a loaf of bread; the soldiers keeping them in order. The soldiers wanted us to take some bread; but we told them we had just had some breakfast, that we did not need it.

A poor woman threw a bag of oranges into our wagon. These came in good for the sick whom we met on the train. You would scarcely know us we have been so black and dirty, no time to think of appearances. Here as in San Francisco, the streets are filled with bricks, etc. It is awful, but poor San Francisco, wicked San Francisco, was well chastened by fire. Oh, God's hand is in it all. Many were trying to keep the people and children good, but oh the vices of the city prevailed and all good people predicted some awful calamity. It has come and all like whipped children bow humbly down, acknowledging God's justice.

Millionaires are poor men today. Castles are gone up in flames; the beautiful hills, so green and fresh, are covered black with people. Our parishioners are all south of [Mount St. Joseph's]. Some of the older Sisters — Mary Alice, Angelica, Robertine and Stanislaus W. — are at [Mount St. Joseph's]. I told them to go down to the camps and comfort the poor people. Sister Mary and Sister Carmelite are safe and quiet at [Mount St. Joseph's] and seem not to want to leave it. If pestilence follows this scourge, God help us. Fortunately the flames consumed hundreds of the dead under the ruins. A few feet back of us on Minna Street, a big hotel caved in and buried two hundred. An unfortunate house of Negroes and whites next to us on Minna was crushed to the earth, everybody in it killed!! Lord have mercy upon them. Oh, God is ever mindful of those who try to serve Him. Praise be His Holy Name!

Mother dearest, this is the time for our dear Community to stand by the Archbishop. Leave us in the city to work wherever we are needed. We will have to begin as the good Sisters in [1852]. Naturally, I would love to go east for I can never get over this shock; but then again, I get brave and want to remain here to comfort my dear Sisters who have been so true, so devoted to me. And I must hunt up our poor little ones and comfort the discouraged parents. I am a pretty good preacher and I'll do some good among the people who have been very devoted.

We just heard that fire has again broken out in San Francisco. It was under control when we left yesterday. Twenty-five patients are just coming in here [hospital in San Jose]; we will be busy. I'll forget my own ills in serving them. Poor little Sister Victorine is wonderfully calm under the great trial. Indeed, everybody is calm and resigned, all back to our primitive simplicity. Oh, God is wonderful! The glorious marble altar is useless; the Holy Sacrifice is offered in the open air, "God's first temples."

Don't worry about us; we are left to do good. The chastening rod has done us all good, all who have felt it. Some have not felt it as hard as others. God knows best! Priests are doing great work for souls; God protect them. I tried to send you a telegram, but could not do so until yesterday. A Priest took it to Oakland and I hope it has reached you. Fond, devoted love [sent] to you from each of the Sisters who all love and appreciate our dear Community more than anything on earth. Love to dear Father Sullivan. I'll write him later; you will please tell him something of this rambling letter. God keep you all from the horrors of earthquake and fire. Don't worry about us; we will get on okay. We are not maimed and crushed as are hundreds. We left all our good habits and linen in the flames. When a Sister comes to me crying about her good habit, I have to laugh at her.

It takes God to strip us of every toy attachment. I feel that never again will I look for anything earthly. Leave us, Mother, to carry on good work in the humbled, crushed city. All hearts are now disposed to do good. My heart to you!

Your devoted daughter,

Sister Eugenia Garvey, U.D.o.C.S.o.t.P.S.
[On Mission at St. Vincent's School,
South of Market]

Love to our dear Officers and Sisters of our dear Mother House,
                    Sister Eugenia

My hand trembles too much to write well.

ST. VINCENT CONVENT—MISSION ST. NEAR THIRD.

*Already our house was on fire, and a
policeman and Father Horan, our good friend, led
us through the surging mass of humanity.
On our sidewalk a crazed bull was goring a man to
death; soon, however, the animal was killed.*

—SISTER EUGENIA GARVEY

In the book *Denial of Disaster,* Gladys Hansen relates the eyewitness accounts of those who saw longhorn steers running loose on the streets of downtown San Francisco just after the earthquake: Dr. Topham of St. Mary's Hospital saw dead steers on Mission and Second; Mr. Roche, a postal worker, saw steers stampeding on Mission and Fremont; Police Officer Walsh also saw steers stampeding on Mission and Fremont, and after shooting down one steer, he witnessed another gore a man to death.

SOURCE: *Denial of Disaster* by Gladys Hansen and others; published by Cameron and Company, San Francisco, 1989; pages 49–54.

THOUSANDS WAIT IN BREAD LINES

People who, a week ago, would have grumbled if the baker's wagon was late, or if the bread was stale, or if the loaf was not of the particular variety they preferred, stood in the bread lines yesterday with hundreds ahead of them and awaited their turn.

The poor and the prosperous were mingled, and all were cheerful. Some ate their bread as they walked along the street; others took it to their home or temporary shelters.

ALL MAIL HELD AT LOCAL OFFICE

Postmaster Fisk has established temporary headquarters in the Oakland Federal building, at Broadway and Seventeenth street. He announces that all mail addressed to San Francisco is being sent there as usual, but is being held there. In order to correct the popular impression that all mail s being sent to Oakland, he particularly desires to call attention to the fact that no San Francisco mail is received there. Those who want theri mail delvered there or elsewhere can attain that end by applying at the Oakland or other postoffices for transfer blanks in the usual course. This alone will insure its delivery.

SOLDIERS MAKE ALL MEN WORK

The soldiers and the police forced every available man in the down-town district of the city to work yesterday, no matter where they were found or under what conditions. One party of four men that came down town in an automobile were stopped on Market street by the soldiers. The well-dressed men were ordered out of the machine and compelled to assist in clearing the debris from Market street so that provisions may be hauled up through the center of the city. Then the automobile was loaded with provisions and sent out to relieve the hungry people in the park.

SAN FRANCISCO CHRONICLE
San Francisco, Sunday, April 22, 1906

50

SIXTY WERE ENTOMBED IN ONE HOTEL

South of Market street the loss of life was mostly brought about by the collapsing of many cheap and crowded lodging-houses. Among others, the caving-in of the Royal, corner Fourth and Minna streets, added to the horror of the situation by the shrieks of its many scores of victims embedded in the ruins and who were unable to escape from the mass of timbers which buried them. Insistently they implored for help, apparently even in their agony realizing that the fire was close upon them. Many of the more fortunate who had escaped from surrounding houses worked hard to liberate the victims before it became too late. As the fire crept steadily onward the shrieks still continued until in despair the rescuers were forced back.

The collapsing of the Portland House, on Sixth street between Mission and Market, came about in a similar manner. Fully sixty persons were entombed midst the crash of timbers and brick, their agonizing cries for relief being heard half a block away.

40 BODIES FROM ONE BUILDING

Forty bodies were taken from the building at 119 Fifth street yesterday by the Red Cross service. The structure, which was a four-story wooden building containing three flats of ten rooms each, collapsed during the earthquake. At the time several persons were taken alive from the upper stories, but it was thought that all the inmates had escaped. The ruins took fire shortly after and, although efforts were made to extinguish the flames, the entire building was consumed. The bodies of the unfortunates imprisoned within the ruins were incinerated, only the skulls and a few bones being left.

SAN FRANCISCO EXAMINER
San Francisco, Sunday, April 22, 1906

water-pipe rendering it impossible to
extinguish the flames. All was truck,
earthquake, fire, no water, the people
all rushing out to the park or towards
our hills. Our Sisters at St. Vincent's
School saw the most of everything, they
no doubt, have given you a better
account than I can. About ten o'clock
they all came out, we felt so sorry for
them but thanked God they were

Sister Genevieve Johnson

[Mount St. Joseph's
San Francisco, California]
April 23, 1906

My very dear Sister,

*T*he grace of Our Lord be with us forever!

When this reaches you, we beg that you say with us a fervent "Deo Gratias." We know that many a fervent prayer has ascended for us from the quiet beloved St. Joseph's and that you will help us to thank our good God who has spared us in every way from the disasters that have fallen around us.

Your Easter wishes reached us today—no need to tell you that they were delayed and Sister Stanislaus R. wishes me to write immediately and tell you about the past week. So, after a hurried "thank you," I shall try to give just a little account concerning ourselves.

On Tuesday evening we received word that we would have no Mass on Wednesday morning as our Chaplain had to sing a Requiem in the Church. As we usually take our weekly long sleep when there is no Mass in the house, Sister Mary Joseph told us to take it on Wednesday instead of Saturday. At 5:15 while we were dressing, there occurred a violent shock of earthquake. The pictures turned around, some statues fell and the shaking of the whole house is truly indescribable. It seemed so providential that we were with the children and could hurry out to them and calm them. Some were very much frightened, others hardly awoke. There seemed to be a dreadful crashing and we thought the building was certainly falling, but only a little plastering fell here and there. When we entered the Chapel, we found every candlestick, every vase and flowers on the floor. It looked dreadful, but no statue in the Chapel had fallen; that of the Sacred Heart tilted and leaned back against the wall. Sister Martina and I straightened the pedestal before the other Sisters were in.

These facts seem calm and nothing compared to what followed. We knew nothing of what was going on in the city. We simply knew that the shock was violent and thought that it must have demolished some buildings; but scarcely were our prayers ended when we heard that many buildings were destroyed, lives lost and that fire had broken out from one end of the city to the other. From our windows we could see the smoke, but thought half of what we heard was exaggeration. Alas, it was too true; the severity of the earthquake broke the main water pipe, rendering it impossible to extinguish the flames. All was [true]: earthquake, fire, no water, the people all rushing out to the park or towards our hills.

Our Sisters at St. Vincent's School saw the worst of everything and they no doubt have given you a better account than I can. About ten o'clock, they all came out; we felt so sorry for them, but thanked God they were saved. At present Sisters Mary Alice, Angelica, Robertine, Stanislaus W., Carmelite, Avellina and Mary are with us. Sister Eugenia and the others are in San Mateo. In the afternoon, all the Sisters and children of the Technical School came out, as they were in danger of the fire. At present Sister Rufina and most of the children are with us. The other Sisters and a few of their large girls returned to their House, which is now safe, to make clothes for the destitute.

To return to the scene of disaster—the fire raged more or less from Wednesday morning until Friday, some few fires even until Sunday morning. Most of the Churches are destroyed, some by the earthquake but the greater number by fire. Dear Sister, it would be impossible to tell you all. Some of our Sisters have seen the ruins of our beautiful city and say they can think of nothing but the destruction of Jerusalem.

But for the bright side—the order and energy of the civil and military authorities and the cheerfulness of the afflicted people are beyond expectation. Before the ashes were cold, they had some arrangements made for reconstruction. While writing the last sentence a slight shock was felt. We had and still have many such, but none have amounted to anything.

Last Sunday, Mass was said all over the city in the open air, but again we were favored and allowed to celebrate the Holy Sacrifice in our Chapel. People are not allowed to make a fire until the chimneys are pronounced safe; the cause of some fires that occurred was damaged chimneys. With us everything is the same as ever; our sorrow is for others. We feel that we cannot be grateful enough to our good God. Many boarding houses were crushed and the inmates sent into eternity in an instant. There is so much to be told, but I leave to others who witnessed it to give you a more graphic description.

Our good Father Glass, as soon as he heard of the disaster, hastened to us and with great difficulty obtained entrance into our city. He came simply to give aid, spiritual or temporal, to see if his Sisters wanted either. He heard the confessions of all, Sisters and girls (that is, those girls who made their First Communion). We have everything we need, thank God.

Our dear Sister Stanislaus R. all through has been so calm and resigned, but of course is very much weaker. Today she is unable to rise at all and our dear Lord went to her in Holy Communion as she could not come to Him. Sister Mary Joseph is also most edifying and calm and is here, there and everywhere, doing all that she can.

Remember us all with loving wishes to our Superiors and dear Sisters, with affectionate remembrance,

Sister Genevieve [Johnson], U.D.O.C.S.O.t.P.S.
[On Mission at Mount St. Joseph's, Silver Terrace]

P.S. April 24th, Sister Eugenia and the rest of her Sisters came here last night after many tribulations [and] like St. Paul passing through fire and water. Thank God, they are all safe here now. We had quite a severe shock of earthquake again last night. Pray much for us, dear Sister, that our good God will continue His protection over our two large Houses of little ones. *S. G.*

ARCHBISHOP AT ST. MARY'S.

On the steps of St. Mary's Cathedral and on the upheaved pavement of Van Ness avenue overlooking the blackened waste that began just across the street Archbishop Montgomery celebrated mass at 8 o'clock. The service was attended by thousands, covering the church steps and extending well up and down the street in either direction. The archbishop's words of comfort and his reference to the death of Fire Chief Sullivan affected the entire great assemblage, and tears streamed down hundreds of the faces upturned to the tiny altar in the open doorway of the vestibule, while the broken sobs swept in a wave of sound from end to end of the congregation.

Archbishop Montgomery said in part:

"San Francisco shall have a day of resurrection. Not a city in the United States destroyed by fire has failed to grow up a better city upon the ruins of the old, and so will San Francisco. Its position is such and the position of California at large is such that it has to be so.

"We must arouse in ourselves that true American spirit that looks not at the city in its devastation, but rather to its day of resurrection.

SAN FRANCISCO EXAMINER
San Francisco, Monday, April 23, 1906

with gratitude for our Providential
protection, not a child nor
Sister received even a scratch,
but escaped with a dreadful
fright, not yet over, as slight
shocks continue to keep us in
alarm. Our walls are badly crack
ed, plastering and chimneys
down. no gas, nor fires allowed
in the city, all cooking is done
in the streets, our kitchen chimneys was kindly repaired or rather
entirely rebuilt, by the men em-

Sister Mary Caine

My very dear Sister,

*T*he grace of Our Lord be with us forever!

Our dear Sister Mary's right hand is somewhat stiff and swollen from over taxing it, so [she] is unable to write herself. She desires me to assure you that she sent a telegram at once, as soon as possible, informing of the safety of our Sisters and children; but some days after, the telegrams were returned as all wire communication was broken. We made several attempts later to dispatch from neighboring suburbs, but without success. On Saturday last, Sister Mary sent special dispatches to the relations of the Sisters of this House; but it seems they are all held en route on account of damaged lines.

I regret that our dear Mother should be made unnecessarily anxious, but Sister Eugenia must have gotten her dispatch off before we were aware of the seriousness of the damage. We thought all as safe as ourselves until their arrival at our House in a body on Wednesday. Conflagrations were then just commencing and raged for three days and nights. Thirteen magnificent Churches with their entire Congregations, large parishes, were completely wiped out. Hotels, business blocks of brick and stone were destroyed, entailing terrible loss of life. The water supply was cut off by the severing of the water pipes by the earthquake, so that the firemen with all their modern apparatus were forced to stand idly by watching the roaring flames. When it became evident that the entire city would be consumed, recourse was had to dynamiting the buildings to stop the progress of the flames and without much success.

Nearly all the other Communities are burned out and are homeless, scattered throughout the city, laboring to relieve the thousands of sufferers of the terrible disaster. When we see the wholesale destruction of property and number the victims by death, our hearts are filled with gratitude for our providential protection; not a child or Sister received even a scratch, but escaped with a dreadful fright not yet over as slight shocks continue to keep us in alarm.

Our walls are badly cracked, plastering and chimneys down; no gas or fires allowed in the city, all cooking is done in the streets. Our kitchen chimneys were kindly repaired, or rather entirely rebuilt, by the men employed in the tunnel who volunteered their services; so we have our meals very comfortably. Provisions of all kinds are abundantly supplied, so there is no danger of famine.

These two [orphanages] are Relief Stations. Thousands come daily for food, clothing, bedding, etc., and are [well] supplied. The children are the worse off, for little provision in clothing for them has arrived. We shelter and feed forty boys from the Youth's Directory, now in ruins. And daily we see the millionaires of last week and the poor man side by side waiting at Relief Stations for a loaf of bread and some other article of food or clothing, and gratefully receiving it for themselves and families.

Nearly a hundred new-born infants are in parks and barns with their poor Mothers without the slightest provisions of clothing, etc. God only knows the sufferings and misery of our once prosperous city. Father Glass, from St. Vincent's College, Los Angeles, came up on Sunday last and brought money to supply the urgent necessities of our different Houses. We received $500, which Sister Mary accepted as a loan and will hold in case of necessity. It was truly kind and thoughtful of him and unasked. May God reward him! Our Sisters take turns in visiting, comforting and relieving the sick victims of our terrible disaster. No pen can adequately describe the sad condition of our city, bodies buried under collapsed buildings and then consumed by fire. No fires occurred out our direction, but we have been obliged to supply the village with water from our reservoir; but God will provide and protect us.

Our children are very good and very earnest in prayers. All unite in affectionate remembrance to you and are most grateful for prayers to preserve our dear Sister Mary during this sad time. She is so engaged in relieving the sufferers that she forgets and neglects her own health, which keeps us anxious for her. She never rests and we fear her nights are anxious and sleepless. Our Sisters are on sentinel duty all night as the city is without light and we are obliged to use night lamps and fear fire. May Our Lord preserve us from further accidents of all kinds! Everyone rejoices that we have thus far escaped serious damage to buildings; but as the shocks of earthquake are renewed each day, although not severe, we are in constant dread.

Our dear Sister Frederica is greatly unnerved, but tries to appear calm and comforts us by her fervent prayers and confidence in Divine Providence. May Our Lord preserve her to us for many years as a model child of St. Vincent!

Please remember us affectionately to our dear Sisters at Home and beg a continuance of their fervent prayers, for we fear all danger of shocks is not yet over as we had one today about noon. A letter with particulars of our condition was mailed to our dear Mother on Thursday week ago. A letter has also been sent to Father Sullivan, but we hear there is some interruption in mail delivery.

> With renewed thanks for prayers,
> I am devotedly,
>
> *Sister Vincentia [Halligan]*, U.D.O.C.S.O.t.P.S.
> [On Mission at Mount St. Joseph
> Infant Asylum, Silver Terrace]

*No pen can adequately describe the
sad condition of our city, bodies
buried under collapsed buildings
and then consumed by fire.*

—Sister Vincentia Halligan

South of Market Ruins

In the book *Denial of Disaster*, Gladys Hansen tells of people trapped in collapsed buildings and consumed by fire: in more than thirty buildings in the South of Market area; and in the Valencia Street Hotel in the Mission District.

SOURCE: *Denial of Disaster* by Gladys Hansen and others; published by Cameron and Company, San Francisco, 1989; pages 18–25.

San Jose

Letters

*written by the Sisters
from the Mission
in San Jose*

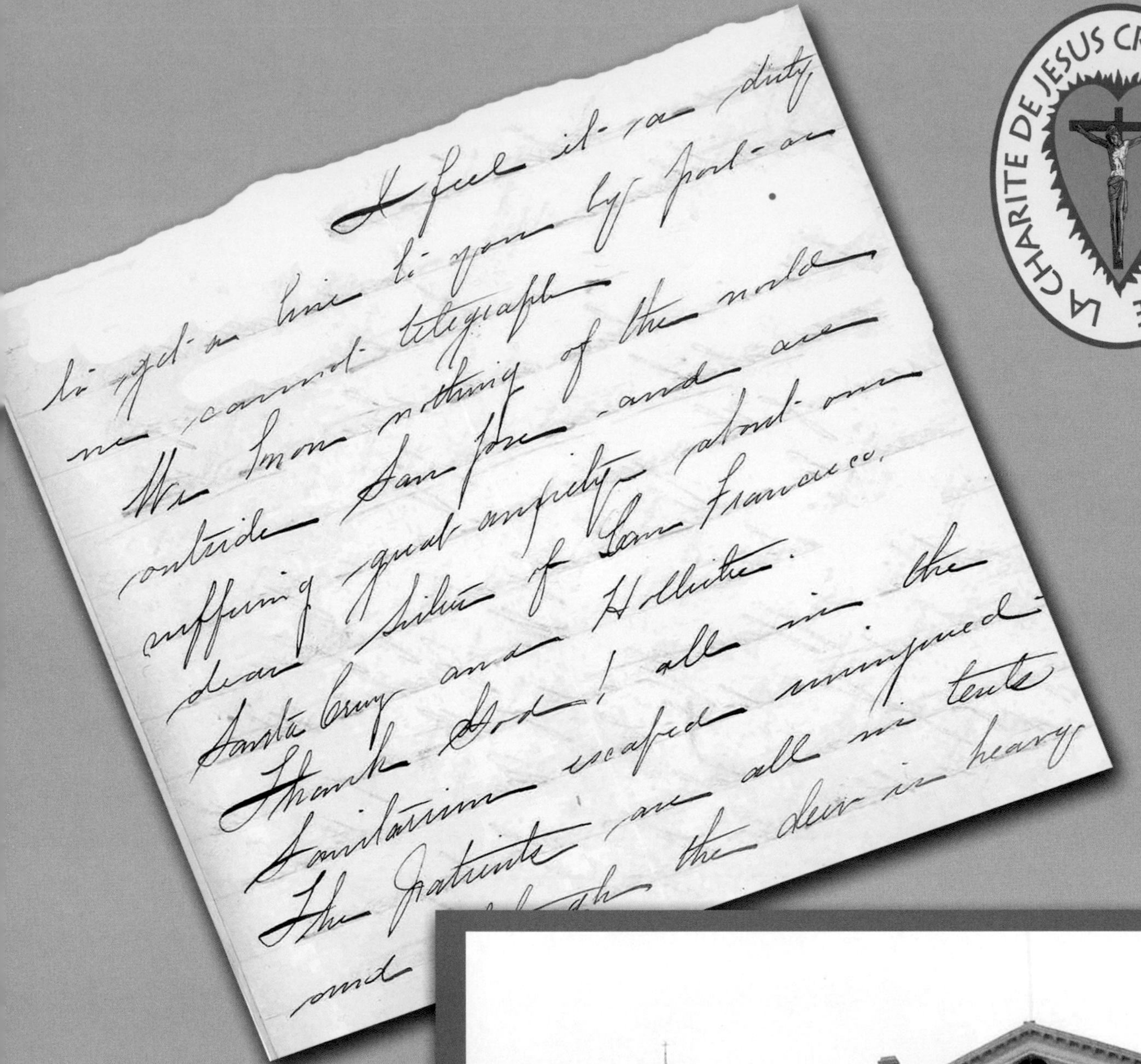

O'Connor Sanitarium
Race and San Carlos
Streets, San Jose

[O'Connor Sanitarium]
San Jose, California
April 19, 1906

My very dear Mother,

*T*he grace of Our Lord be with us forever!

I feel it a duty to get a line to you by post as we cannot telegraph. We know nothing of the world outside San Jose and are suffering great anxiety about our dear Sisters of San Francisco, Santa Cruz and Hollister.

Thank God, all in the Sanitarium escaped uninjured. The patients are all in tents and although the dew is heavy, they all seem cheerful and comfortable. The building is badly damaged and is unsafe. The first dreadful shock nearly swept us into eternity. The large Chapel was nearly demolished. I could only think that the God Whom we call our Spouse [is] a terrible God. When we recovered our equilibrium, we found all the inmates unharmed. The roof fell in here and there on the beds which were empty. One of the girls was saved by a miracle when the laundry chimney fell in on her bed. We pushed the debris sufficiently out of the way in the Sanctuary to have Mass in thanksgiving for our delivery, climbing over the rubbish to Holy Communion.

After breakfast there were a few light shakings. Then about 2:30 P.M. another shock, when I felt it a duty to order everyone out of the buildings. While patients slept in tents during the night, the House received still greater injury which renders it unsafe to enter. All the beds and furniture are being moved out and we will try with God's help to fix comfortable shelter in boarded tents. I hardly know just what will be done, but our hearts are ready to start anew. A few of the Sisters are extremely nervous, but are keeping up bravely.

Dear Mother, please have some special prayers offered for these really noble old people, Mr. and Mrs. O'Connor; their faults are offset by great virtue. Sister Dolores' leg was slightly bruised by falling plaster in the Chapel. Sister Fidelis' hands were scratched by broken glass which fell all around her. No one else was injured.

The place is under martial law. The people are terrified. We are beside ourselves with anxiety about the other Sisters in California. Pardon all my mistakes. Pray to God for us.

Very obediently in Our Lord,

Sister M. Victorine [Fitzgerald],
U.D.O.C.S.O.T.[Sick Poor]
[On Mission at O'Connor Sanitarium, San Jose]

[P.S.] We had Mass this morning in the front vestibule; the house trembled several times. The night dews are heavy, the mid-day sun is hot. Pray our Lord to spare the Sisters. We have plenty of help.

Sister Victorine Fitzgerald
O'Connor Sanitarium

STATE HOSPITAL AT AGNEW IS IN RUINS

No Less Than One Hundred and Twenty-Five Inmates Killed.

Several Physicians, Nurses and Attendants Slain.

Mercury and Herald
San Jose, California, Thursday Afternoon, April 19, 1906

[O'Connor Sanitarium]
San Jose, California
April 24, 1906

My dear Mother,

*T*he grace of Our Lord be with us forever!

All here continue in good health. The heavy rain has necessitated moving the patients. The Doctor at the Emergency Hospital (a large two-story shed for packing fruit) has given the upper story and cots sufficient to accommodate our sick ones. The Homers we have in the barn and in snug tents here with us. Two Sisters and two nurses remained with the patients last [night], Sister Mary Rose and Sister Teresa, and this morning Sister Mary Alice and Sister Agnes relieved them. The rain caused much discomfort and confusion, but things are much better since the patients are well sheltered. The Doctor anticipates giving one hundred patients to the Sisters' Department should they arrive from the city.

We are getting one end of the House, which is perfectly safe, under roof. The fire can be lit in the kitchen and laundry; masons have arranged everything safely. We have a nice clean shed put up on the front barn with tar paper over it and I think we are very comfortable. It is wet, but no one seems to be taking cold. Sister Dolores is still limping, but her bruise is not severe. I wish I could tell you something definite about the plans of the O'Connors for the future.

The architects assure us [that] parts of the building are safe, but must be "bonded," i.e., be braced with iron in the weak parts. The annex building is badly damaged; the carpenters are bracing the walls up with wooden beams to keep them from falling. They hope to be able to save the floor of the operating rooms by using "jacks" from the foundation to the tiled floors. I suppose the wall will be put up piece by piece. They seem to know all about it, but I can only listen for I do not understand. The kitchen, laundry, servants' rooms and all the north wing seem to be safe; they are trying to get it under roof for us at once.

Mrs. O'Connor has pencil and paper drawing plans for a wooden wing to extend onto the orchard, moving the cottage to the end of the future wing. I will not tell you anything further because she may change her plans tomorrow. The Blessed Sacrament is still kept in the Chapel, but Mass is offered in the parlor. The Chapel building will be saved, but it must be repaired. Great fears are entertained about the population of San Francisco, but all this is only anticipating evil. Exposure and dampness may cause much sickness; I will write as definitely as I can.

When I look around me, I wonder if we will ever be orderly and tidy again. Please write and tell me if you do not approve of the hospital arrangement. We will probably get into the rooms in the north wing in ten days. Shall we withdraw them from the other places or shall I leave a Sisters' Department there should their services be needed? I will, of course, be very careful. This has been a fearful ordeal. But the terrible rain on the patients has caused more anxiety and confusion than even the earthquake. How I wish someone could come here with authority from you. I would feel much more confidence in planning; it is impossible for me to explain. I am going down to the depot. The people have asked for a Sister to take charge of the Stray Children's Department.

Please pray for us, dear Mother.

Yours in obedience,

Sister M. Victorine [*Fitzgerald,*
U.D.o.C.S.o.t.S.P.
On Mission at O'Connor Sanitarium,
San Jose]

EMERGENCY HOSPITAL.

There Is Systematic Organization and All the Numerous Patients Are Being Well Cared For.

At the Emergency Hospital, in the Chilton warehouse on North First street, everything is being carried on in an orderly way. Wards have been arranged. The corps of attendants have been organized systematically and patients from the desolated districts of San Francisco are being cared for as rapidly as they arrive.

Although the train service between Oakland, San Francisco and San Jose has not yet been placed back to schedule, early morning trains arrived in this city today and others left for points to the south. A large number of refugees that were driven from their temporary shelter in San Francisco, came to San Jose this morning. None were seriously injured, but all were worn out and few had sufficient clothing to protect them from the cold drizzle of rain that began shortly after 3 o'clock this morning. Those of the San Franciscans who were injured were treated at once at the Emergency Hospital. The baggage trucks were piled high with the personal effects of the refugees, mostly clothing tied up in a quilt or a counterpane.

San Jose Herald
San Jose, California, Monday Afternoon, April 23, 1906

[O'Connor Sanitarium]
San Jose, California
April 27, 1906

My dear Sister Eugenia,

*T*he grace of Our Lord be with us forever!

Your kind letter received. You have heard by this time that all our Sisters are safe. The people are still laboring under great excitement; indeed this disaster was enough to cause even greater confusion. We are getting back gradually into the northwest wing, but the rain is pouring in everywhere. Much of the building will be unfit for use for a long time; the people will dread to be sick and helpless in a two-story brick house.

Mrs. O'Connor has the architect drawing plans for a one-story frame wing, which will be put up immediately, and after this the repairs will begin. The whole annex has been almost destroyed; they have the walls propped up with wooden beams. The patients are located temporarily in a large store house downtown; it is a two-story wooden shed which has been converted into a temporary emergency hospital. The Doctor in charge has given the Sisters the upper story.

The heavy rain following so quickly has caused the greatest confusion and discomfort. All our patients were in tents on our grounds, but we were obliged to move them. We have a shed with tar paper roof for a dormitory. The Sisters are keeping well; sleeping out-of-doors seems to agree with them; but, of course, our unsettled condition beggars description. Sister Aloysia and I will sleep in the house tonight for the first time as we have the old folks indoors at last. The Sisters are still timid and no one could blame them, for we have had a very terrifying experience. I sat perfectly still, but I was sure the walls of the Chapel would fall in and bury us alive. I thought, Jesus, Master, I am just where it is your will for me to be; and then again, my gentle Jesus is such a terrible God! The earth is still trembling and we are having thunder, wind and rain. It seems impossible for the elements to settle again into peace. Pray for us, dear Sister.

Your,

Sister M. Victorine [Fitzgerald],
U.D.o.C.S.o.t.S.P.
[On Mission at O'Connor Sanitarium,
San Jose]

Hollister and Santa Cruz

Letters

written by the Sisters
from the Missions in
Hollister and Santa Cruz

SACRED HEART SCHOOL
Sixth and West Streets, Hollister

How Can I write of the dreadful thing that has happened to poor Cauij? There can be no exageration in the statements which the account can be put in print. Port Hollister did not escape our house is demolished how we came out of the house alive is a mystery not only to those who see the condition of the place

[Sacred Heart School]
Hollister, California
April 19, 1906

My dear Mother,

*T*he grace of Our Lord be with us forever!

How can I write of the dreadful thing that has happened to poor California? There can be no exaggeration in the statements when the account can be put in print. Poor Hollister did not escape. Our House is demolished. How we came out of the House alive is a mystery, not only to those who see the condition of the place but to ourselves. The Sisters proved themselves most courageous, going to the third floor for the children, plaster falling around them and blinding and smothering them at every step. Sister Mary Angela was most calm; strange too, for at smaller shocks in the past [she] would be greatly frightened.

I did not go to the third floor. At the third shock about 5:10 A.M., I left the Chapel to go to the [dormitory], to the children on the second floor; but only got as far as the clothes room where I met a girl who fell at almost every step. Then plastering began to fall on us; we went down the front stairs which were swinging [under us and] with difficulty we reached the front porch. It must have been then that the House was thrown from its foundation and about four feet to the right of its former position, for I was thrown to the ground from the porch steps. I felt very cowardly, Mother, but I did not have the courage to reenter the building. The Sisters were inside bringing the eleven with them.

The House is in a most frightful condition. We have rented a cottage which we will use for a school to keep the children with us, and we will live in another a short distance away. You will tell us, dear Mother, what to do. The people are in distress, fearing the Sisters will be taken from them. The people I feel will help to rebuild the place. We were told today that they may be able to raise the building and brace and build a new foundation, but there is nothing definite yet. We have been trying to get out the furniture.

You do not know how badly we felt when Father Smyth came to take the Blessed Sacrament away. The Church suffered very little, but some of the important buildings have been destroyed; two persons were killed and others injured. We went last evening to visit the wounded at the Sanitarium here and to console the family of the lady who was killed instantly.

Dear Mother, you will pardon this miserable scratch and the poor account I have written. Since I [began writing] this, we have had another shock. They continued all day. Yesterday, last night, we had six. We are not as badly off as they are in San Francisco. We had no fire.

Pray for us. The Sisters all unite in love and sorrow in sending love.

I am, dear Mother, your devoted child,

Sister Teresa Hill, U.D.o.C.S.o.t.P.S.
[On Mission at Sacred Heart School, Hollister]

HOLLISTER IS STRICKEN WITH FEARFUL FORCE

Buildings Are Tumbled Into Masses of Awful Debris.

Five Are Killed and Many Injured---Property Loss Heavy.

The Sacred Heart Convent on Sixth street was shaken off its foundation and moved four feet north. The building is three stories high, and the little children who board there were sleeping in the third room dormitory. Although in peril of their lives, as the plaster was falling and the stairs were caving in, the brave sisters in charge succeeded in getting the little children safely down.

MERCURY AND HERALD
San Jose, California,
Thursday Afternoon, April 19, 1906

My very dear Sister,

*T*he grace of Our Lord be with us forever!

How good it seemed to get a word from "Home." I haunted the telegraph office every day, but could get my message off no sooner; you no doubt have it ere this. We got an awful shaking; I made for the children's dormitories, and the stairs, banisters and wall and I came in close contact before I reached the top; and on reaching the last step a heavy cornice fell, just grazing the cornette. The dear children, reassured by the presence of a Sister, became calm, but didn't they pray! I shuddered when I looked down into their playground; a mass of bricks from the chimneys marked the spot where many would have been killed had the quake come a little later. I tried to get all of our Sisters by phone, but only succeeded in getting Sister Teresa, who told us they were leveled.

As soon as an architect examined our building and found foundation and framework perfectly sound, another Sister and I went over to Hollister. Even for that short distance the sights were appalling; we were on the first train that had ventured over the road. Here and there on repaired places the telegraph poles were about three feet high, showing how deep the earth had sunk. Again on the mountains the huge boulders and uprooted trees had stopped half way down in the landslide. We got out and walked over the trestles of the bridges.

We found Hollister almost in ruins, our Sisters' House one of the worst. It had moved four feet to the north, every seam is asunder, the kitchen dropped into the cellar; it was indeed demolished. That the Sisters and children escaped with their lives is miraculous; just after the last little [one] was brought out in night clothes, a pile of bricks closed up the passage behind them. The porch sank as they stepped on it and the other end rose and gave them a good bump. The Sisters were thrown to the floor in the Chapel, and when they picked themselves up and got to the door, they found it wedged; by superhuman strength they pulled it open and it fell on them. Was it not awful! We helped them move their furniture from some rooms where they were allowed to enter; and then finding we [could] give no more assistance and that no one would accept our invitation to come home with us, we left them living quite in the primitive style. I heard their Pastor tell them he would bring them the Blessed Sacrament if they fitted up a place for it.

On our way home we boarded a train of refugees from San Francisco; they were nice, refined people, but disheveled from their hurried flight and exposure. They had had no breakfast; so when the good country people entered the train at the station and served them with milk and sandwiches, they ate like people who were really hungry. We were served like the rest; but on explaining that we had had a good breakfast, we turned over our portion to our neighbor.

We have had repeated small shocks every day and night since; even today quite a shock alarmed everyone. We have not had our clothes off for several nights, for the children are so nervous and fearful that we are afraid of a panic.

The eyewitnesses, who are pouring in here every day, say no tongue or pen could tell the horrors of that night there in San Francisco. These are the Churches and Schools that are destroyed: [Churches] St. Ignatius, Notre Dame, St. Joseph's, St. Brendan's, St. Francis, St. Boniface, St. Mary's, Paulist, St. Patrick's, St. Rose's, St. Pietro and Paulo, Our Lady of Guadalupe; [Schools, etc.] Holy Names Convent, Notre Dame, Presentation, Sacred Heart College, Sacred Heart Presentation Convent, St. Vincent's, St. Patrick's, Youth's Directory and St. Mary's Hospital. [O'Connor] Sanitarium is damaged; the Sisters are camping on their lawn.

Now dear Sister, help us to thank God that no lives under our charge were lost. Sister Stanislaus R. lives through it all; her House has become a refuge for the Technical girls (their house was not destroyed and is being used for the destitute) and St. Vincent's Sisters. The Sisters are going in wagons to attend the sick in the different camps.

Thank our dear Sisters for sympathy and prayers. Some of us half expected Father Sullivan would run out.

Yours in our All, a very sleepy Sister,

Sister Helena [McGhan], U.D.O.C.S.O.T.P.S.
[On Mission at Holy Cross School,
Santa Cruz]

REPORT CONDITIONS TO BE GOOD IN SANTA CRUZ

SAN JOSE HERALD
San Jose, California, Friday Afternoon, April 20, 1906

*I shuddered when I looked down into
their playground; a mass of bricks from the
chimneys marked the spot where many would
have been killed had the quake
come a little later.*

—Sister Helena McGhan

Holy Cross School and Orphanage
Emmet and School Streets, Santa Cruz

preceding one. God knows
what is yet to come. Thank
God we had no fire
and have been able to
get furniture clothing etc
from the ruins; we are
huddled in a rented house
and have a little cottage
a short distance away for
a school. Our St. Class
came to us as an Angel
of Consolation and gave us
Spiritual help and also
Material help when we
need it. I

Hollister in Ruins

[Sacred Heart School]
Hollister, California
April 30, 1906

Dear Sister Eugenia,

*T*he grace of Our Lord be with us forever!

Your letter was a great consolation to us. I am glad the telegram reached you so soon. I feared it would not, as we were cut off from everyone. The dreadful shocks still continue; each makes me weaker than the preceding one. God knows what is yet to come. Thank God, we had no fire and have been able to get furniture, clothing, etc., from the ruins. We are huddled in a rented house and have a little cottage a short distance away for a school. Good Father Glass came to us as an Angel of Consolation and gave us spiritual help and also material help when we needed it. I shall never forget his kindness. Sister, we try not to complain, but we are somewhat anxious. Poor St. Vincent's School! But God knows best!

Our Pastor told me to write our account to the Bishop; I did so and received a letter of sympathy from him. He wants me to let him know when we are to rebuild, etc. The Pastor too is anxious to know. I must wait for [word] from Father Sullivan. We have no money and the people will not give much. Should we go in debt, there is no prospect of paying, as we already owe $16,000 to the Community and for support are depending on the board of eleven children and about $120.00 a year from the orchard. You can, dear Sister, understand our situation. I told Father Smyth that I could say nothing until I hear from Emmitsburg. Thank God, we are well and try to be happy. Remember us in your petitions to our Blessed Mother.

[Affectionately] Yours,

Sister Teresa [Hill], U.D.O.C.S.O.T.P.S.
[On Mission at Sacred Heart School,
Hollister]

HOLLISTER SCHOOLS WILL REOPEN ON APRIL 30

SUNDAY MERCURY AND HERALD
San Jose, California, Sunday Morning, April 29, 1906

San Francisco

Memoirs

of the 1906 Earthquake and Fire
shared in later years
by Sister Alexis Kuhn

MARKET STREET

SISTER ALEXIS KUHN

In the book *Denial of Disaster*, Gladys Hansen indicates that the earthquake occurred at 5:12:05 A.M. and that fires broke out in the South of Market area almost immediately afterwards with the Prost's Bakery fire spreading rapidly at 6:15 A.M. from the area of Howard and Sixth. (This was the fire that surrounded St. Vincent's School and the adjacent Sisters' residence.)

SOURCE: *Denial of Disaster* by Gladys Hansen and others; published by Cameron and Company, San Francisco, 1989; pages 13, 18–24, 61.

Account of the Earthquake and Fire
as told by Sister Alexis Kuhn

Sister Alexis was one of the twenty Sisters of Charity staffing [St. Vincent's School and St. Patrick's Boys' School]. All of the Sisters were making morning meditation in the Chapel when the earthquake occurred. Exact clocks showed the onset to be a few seconds after 5:12 A.M.

In the early morning of April 18, 1906, the sleeping city of San Francisco was shocked by a violent earth tremor a few seconds after 5:12. What the quake did not shatter, rampant fire consumed. After four devastating days the proud but fallen city counted: her dead, 450; her loss, $500,000,000; and her damage, 28,000 structures destroyed. Over a quarter of a million homeless men, women and children steeled themselves to the awesome task of rebuilding.

Residences of the entire parish wreckage were swept through by fire the first day. These included: the Church; Priests' House; and two Schools, St. Vincent's and St. Patrick's Boys' School (both conducted by the Daughters of Charity under the supervision of Sister Eugenia Garvey . . . assisted by nineteen companions and five lay teachers). The attendance was 1,000 plus pupils.

A low, heavy sound like thunder, in less than a minute, left nothing erect in the Chapel but a bare altar. We headed for the street, met Father Horan and a fire warden at the front entrance, who directed us to remain in the parlor near the front door, first floor, fearing other shakes would follow. Father Horan, Assistant at the Church, secured the Blessed Sacrament from the Tabernacle in the Chapel on the second floor; we received Holy Communion and were given conditional absolution. This was followed by the request, "Sisters, please follow me." Immediately we did so, for fire had started in the next block. In silence we continued, reached St. Mary's Hospital conducted by Sisters of Mercy about 8:15 A.M. We were served coffee and bread before starting for [Mount St. Joseph's and Mount St. Joseph Infant Asylum], both in the same area, a distance of three miles further south. There was no transportation but to walk.

We reached our goal at 10:45 A.M. The less able went to [Mount St. Joseph] Infant Asylum at the foot of the hill; the others continued and reached [Mount St. Joseph's] at the hilltop about 11:20 A.M. We had dinner and received a sisterly sincere welcome. We followed the order of the afternoon until bedtime. Having a full view of the burning city, the majority, too disturbed to sleep, watched the destructive work of the flames; but the disabled retired.

The large water-mains were broken by the tremor. The Chief of the Fire Department was one of the first victims. The city was in a state of chaos, was now an area of fire. The Pacific Ocean to the West and nine thousand miles wide; the

San Francisco Bay to the Southeast and sixty-five miles long; the Golden Gate Strait to the Northeast and eight miles long (width three miles average)—these were the boundaries of our city, though we could not draw a drop of water.

Very Rev. J. J. Sullivan, Director, arrived ten days after the quake from Emmitsburg. [We] refugees awaited placement at future homes. Four of our number were recalled to Emmitsburg; ten were sent to our nearer Missions on the Pacific Coast. The remaining six awaited the decision of the Archbishop regarding the possibility of rebuilding the school.

Death and destruction were spread over thousands of square miles, over a distance of two hundred miles long, from forty to twenty miles wide. [In San Francisco], the exact number of dead was never certain since the fire swept through before the wreckage could be cleared.

But more of San Francisco was saved than destroyed. The waterfront was intact and ready for business. The homes of one hundred and fifty-thousand were spared. The parks and military installations stood untouched. The question "What if?" meant nothing to the stricken. The real value of the harsh experience gave insight and wisdom to accept "What is."

PLACE OF REFUGE
Mount St. Joseph Infant Asylum at the foot of the hill

April 18, 1906

About ten minutes after the quake, Father Horan, Assistant at St. Patrick's, entered and found us (the entire personnel) in the parlor near the front entrance. He did not stop, but went direct to the Chapel and took the Ciborium from the Tabernacle. He returned to the parlor where he gave a general absolution and we received Holy Communion.

He remarked, "The city is doomed; we must move on." He leading, Ciborium in grip, directed his steps toward St. Mary's Hospital conducted by Sisters of Mercy and located on Rincon Hill. There we had a cup of coffee and bread. At eight o'clock there was a second "Shake" and we left the building and started for the orphanages in San Francisco South. We reached [Mount St. Joseph] Infant Asylum at 11:00 A.M. where we rested until evening. Then the Sisters who had calmed down enough [went to bed], while the remaining five sat watching the progress of the burning city five miles away.

Three days later, Sister Eugenia and her five companions started for the car barn where many victims of the quake were lying on the ground floor receiving first aid through Red Cross nurses and doctors. We offered our assistance for bedside care which we continued for three days, returning to the orphanage each night. A week later we went by train to San Jose, where the patients of the O'Connor Sanitarium had been taken from the unsafe damaged building to the open yard and placed on mattresses. We remained for a week, then returned to the city and became interested in the whereabouts of our parish people.

PLACE OF REFUGE
Mount St. Joseph's at the top of the hill

San Francisco

Letters

written by the Sisters describing the
destruction of Mary's Help Hospital
have never been found

PROPOSED DESIGN DRAWING
Mary's Help Hospital, Guerrero and Brosnan Streets

The cornerstone of Mary's Help Hospital was laid on Guerrero Street in 1903; on April 18, the almost completed hospital was demolished. Guerrero and Brosnan Streets were on the edge of the four-square-mile area of charred ruins. Fires raged to the north and to the east. In the Mission District, fire consumed many dwelling places, while the fire in Hayes Valley spread to the Mechanics Pavilion where the sick and dying were housed.

APRIL 1906
Mary's Help Hospital, Guerrero and Brosnan Streets

BIG FIRE IN MISSION

SAN FRANCISCO, April 18. —A great fire is raging in the Mission district and is utterly beyond control. Before night, it is estimated, that in this particular section of the city 50,000 persons will be homeless.

RESIDENCES BURNING

SAN FRANCISCO, April 18. —An intense fire broke out late this afternoon immediately west of the Mechanics' Pavilion, threatening to destroy one of the most thickly populated residence districts of the city. As there were no fire apparatus on hand the flames are raging unchecked.

THE CALL-CHRONICLE-EXAMINER
San Francisco, Thursday, April 19, 1906

Chapter Three

Recovery and Rebuilding
May ~ August of 1906

Eyewitness Accounts

Letters ~ Notes ~ Memoirs

After four days of earthquake and fire,
a four-square-mile area of the city
of San Francisco lay in charred ruins.
Nothing was left but rubble and steel
frames. Then, the people of
San Francisco began the difficult task
of rebuilding their city.

Aftermath

After four days of earthquake and fire, a four-square-mile area of the city of San Francisco lay in charred ruins. Nothing was left but rubble and steel frames. The relief effort was under way with people sleeping in tents and standing in line for food.

After a few weeks, the recovery effort was under way. St. Vincent's School and St. Patrick's Boys' School were putting up a "temporary school" at Fifth and Clementina Streets that would house them both. The Sisters moved into temporary quarters and opened the school in early August, less than four months after the earthquake and fire.

St. Francis Technical School moved into temporary quarters and leased their building at Gough and Geary to the City for use by the Relief Committee. Three years later, they moved back to their Gough and Geary location and into a new building.

Mary's Help Hospital, after years of litigation, was finally able to rebuild on the same site. In 1912, six years after the earthquake and fire, the new hospital on Guerrero and Brosnan Streets was finally in operation.

The cities outside of San Francisco were also recovering from the earthquake. O'Connor Sanitarium in San Jose was able to rebuild the damaged parts of their hospital (operating room, Chapel, etc.) with a substantial contribution from Myles and Amanda O'Connor. Sacred Heart School in Hollister began rebuilding their school and held classes in tents until November of 1906, when the new classrooms were ready.

San Francisco

Letters

*written by the Sisters
from the Missions
in San Francisco*

Ruins of stately churches an colleges an schools — Gods ways are truly not our but we know — that His ways are the best an thru fire an tribulation His love shines out — I firmly believe that "the darkest hour is the hour before the dawn" an I know that good will come out of all this sorrow. A purified city will arise on the ruins a poor old San Francisco People are still camping on the hills the food supplies which come in are given out by Red Cross Agents to long lines of people eagerly awaiting their portion of bread and soup. The worst part of the trouble

SISTER EUGENIA GARVEY

San Francisco, California
May 1, 1906

Sister Eugenia Fealy, Assistant

My very dear Sister,

*T*he grace of Our Lord be with us forever!

Many thanks for your kind and sympathetic letter! Sisterly affection and sympathy is about the only consolation in the day of trial. Thank you, dearest Sister, for your kindness in offering to supply us with clothes. Today, we recovered some aprons, etc., and two or three habits which we left at a friend's; but hearing that she had been burned out we were sure they were lost. We are delighted to get them back safe and sound. Sister Cecilia, a thin, long-waisted little Sister, sorely needs a habit; she did not recover hers. Also Sister Joannes, she too is a little Sister, but shorter-waisted and a little stouter than Sister Cecilia.

You cannot imagine our joy on seeing our dear Father Sullivan, who reached [Mount St. Joseph's] on last Sunday afternoon to our great surprise and delight. Oh, there is nothing like a glimpse of our dear Superiors when we are in trouble. Our dear Father Sullivan looks wonderfully well, thank God! His presence is a great comfort to us.

I do not know what is to be done with us, for I can't see any work awaiting us here. Four large parishes in our section of the city are completely wiped out of existence. Indeed the entire city is destroyed. Standing on the corner near Mission and Fifth, the eye can detect nothing as far as it can see but ruins, awful charred ruins of once majestic buildings.

About 200,000 people have left the city and I believe that few will ever return to it. All the beauty, the riches and the magnificent climate can never tempt back again the poor creatures who passed through that horrible experience! Oh Sister, even now when the memory of it comes up before me, I grow sick and want to die. It seems as though we had been summoned to judgment and had to return again to continue our exile, only to be called again. I can't forget it for one minute.

On Easter everything was so lovely, holy and peaceful: the beautiful procession of lovely girls and boys walking before the Blessed Sacrament on Holy Thursday; the Tenebrae for the first time in our big Church; the fine singing by our fifty beautiful Altar boys; and at nine o'clock Mass the hundreds and hundreds of boys singing in lovely voice and perfect time the praises of the Risen Savior, calling on all to Rejoice. Ah me, and now only ruins, ruins on all sides: ruins of stately churches and colleges and schools. God's ways are truly not ours, but we know that His ways are the best and through fire and tribulation His love shines out! I firmly believe that "the darkest hour is the hour before the dawn," and I know that good will come out of all this sorrow. A purified city will arise on the ruins of poor old San Francisco.

People are still camping on the hills; the food supplies which come in are given out by Red Cross agents to long lines of people eagerly awaiting their portion of bread and soup. The worst part of the trouble is to come. Our united family must now be separated and our hearts nigh broken. Our dear Father Sullivan is now here. Yesterday, he returned from Hollister.

Please give my love to each dear Officer of the Community and to your own dear self, my love and gratitude.

Yours affectionately in our Lord
and St. Vincent,

Sister Eugenia Garvey, U.D.O.C.S.O.T.P.S.
[On Mission at St. Vincent's School,
South of Market]

[Mount St. Joseph's
San Francisco, California]
May 18, 1906

Mother Margaret,

My own beloved Mother!

*T*he grace of Our Lord be forever with us!

Ere this you have reached "Home, sweet Home" and have received a loving welcome from your devoted Daughters whose prayers follow you wherever you go. I hope that little visit was not marred by any worry about your California children, though I fear that it was. How do you like Puerto Rico? How delighted our dear Sisters must have been to have you with them for a few weeks!

We are sorry that our poor, dear State has lost its good name! No description of "calla lilies, roses and fruit, sunshine and green hills" will ever again tempt an easterner to turn westward. Indeed, I marvel how anybody will remain here who is free to get out of it! I have the same feeling that I would have were I surrounded by the "Boxers" in China. Our lives are just as uncertain.

Our nerves are in a pretty bad state. The memory of the 18th of April and its horrors haunt me day and night. Ever since my terrible experience, I have nightly dreamed that walls and houses are falling upon me! The sight of our ruined city is saddening!

Every Sunday six of our Sisters go into the city (where city used to be) and assist at Mass in a little shed which our Pastor has erected on the corner of Fifth and Clementina Streets, site of our new school. About 300 people gather there. They and the children certainly love the Sisters! Poor people, they have lost everything. Many of them have lost relatives in the catastrophe. Our dear little Sister Estelle is still making inquiries about her poor Mother who has not been heard of since the disaster. Over ten thousand at least were buried beneath the fallen houses and then consumed by the devouring flames. Many thought that it was the end of the world, so terrible was it.

My heart has suffered much in parting with eleven of our dear Sisters. They too, dear Sisters, felt almost broken-hearted, especially dear Sister Joannes (by the way her good Aunt, Mrs. P. of Los Angeles, California, sent us $100.00) and Sister Cecilia. The former went to El Paso and the latter to Detroit Hospital and dear old Sister Angelica went to Boyle Heights, Los Angeles, and Sister Robertine to Los Angeles Infirmary.

We may yet have a good school; children are awaiting us they say. [Archbishop Riordan] insists on us remaining.... I am not the least desirous to stay in

California. How could anybody be after such an experience as we had? Still, I hope for grace to brave the inevitable. My heart is jumping all the time. These little shakes, which are continually occurring, keep one in constant agony.

Our dear Father Sullivan has been our comfort and our strength. God bless him! Our Annual Retreat will close Tuesday. How I dread to see him, our dear Father, leave us!

All of our dear Sisters join me in fond love to you, dearest Mother. In my daily prayers you have a big share, believe me in the love of our Lord and St. Vincent.

Your devoted daughter,

Sister Eugenia Garvey, U.D.o.C.S.o.t.P.S.
[On Mission at St. Vincent's School,
South of Market]

THE DUTY OF THE HOUR

In the face of the appalling calamity which has left San Francisco prostrate in the dust, it becomes the duty of all who have the public ear to sound a note of faith and hope. The extraordinary fortitude and courage displayed by our people under circumstances of direst distress, recalls the best traditions of the intrepid race that laid the foundations of the shattered metropolis. It forestalls the word of cheer on the lips of the most sanguine. We turn therefore without misgiving from the memory of the San Francisco of the pioneers to the vision of the new and greater city destined to emerge from the ashes of the old. The spirit which calmly surveys the present waste with unfaltering optimism and indomitable resolution, is an infallible guarantee of the speedy and complete rehabilitation of our beloved city, commercially, materially and spiritually.

+ P. W. RIORDAN,
Archbishop of San Francisco.

San Francisco Monitor
May 19, 1906

98

Our dear little Sister Estelle is still making inquiries about her poor Mother who has not been heard of since the disaster. Over ten thousand at least were buried beneath the fallen houses and then consumed by the devouring flames.

—SISTER EUGENIA GARVEY

SISTER ESTELLE MURPHY

On the Virtual Museum of the City of San Francisco Web site, Gladys Hansen notes that the number of deaths from the 1906 Earthquake and Fire has reached more than 3,000. She also notes that in the area South of Market, many lodging houses collapsed during the earthquake and then caught fire. She thinks thousands of people may have been buried under the rubble and then consumed by fire. Gladys Hansen continues to gather information to determine the accurate number of deaths from the 1906 Earthquake and Fire.

SOURCE: The Virtual Museum of the City of San Francisco Web site (www.sfmuseum.org).

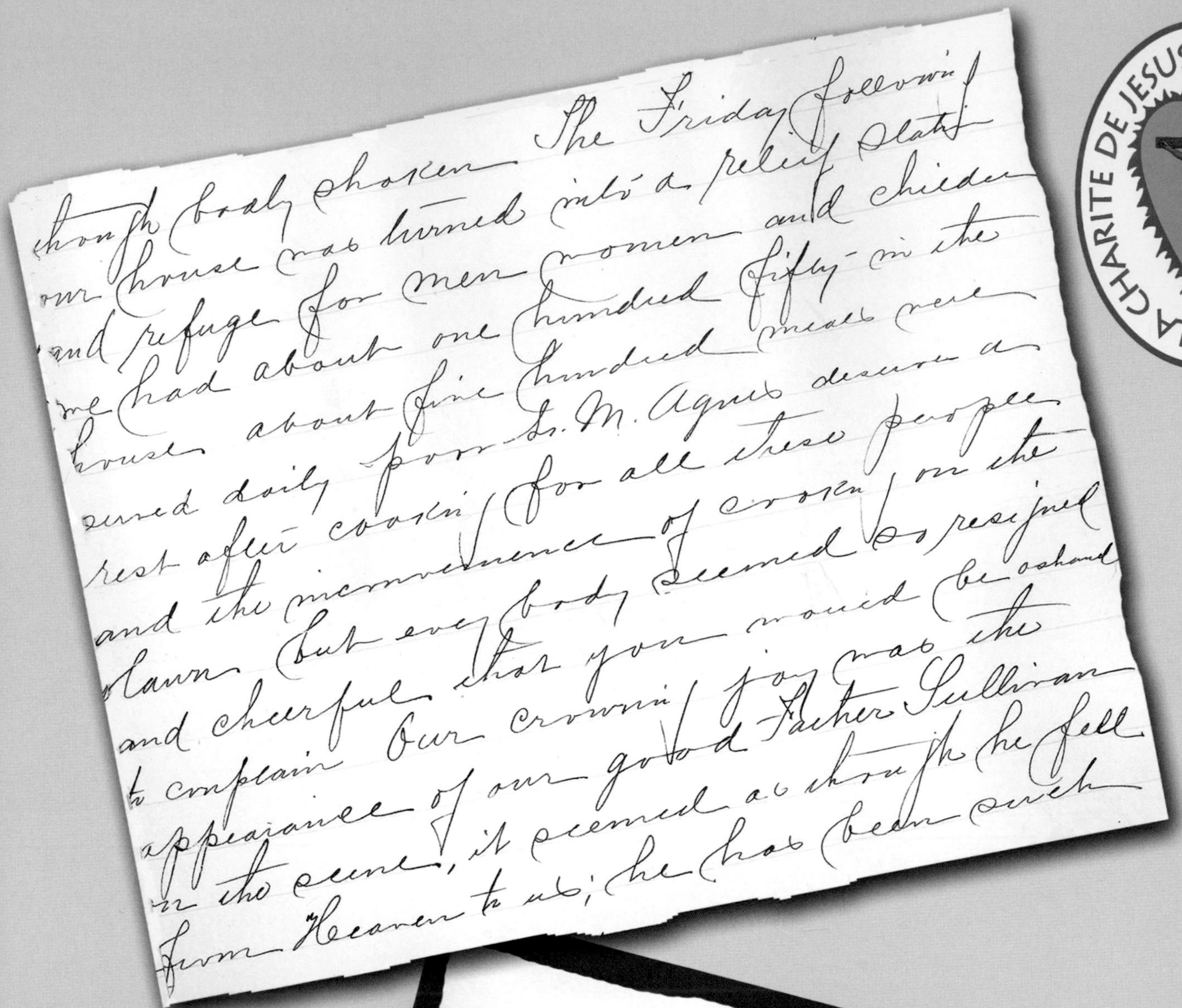

though badly shaken. The Friday following
our house was turned into a relief station
and refuge for men, women and children;
we had about one hundred fifty in the
house, about five hundred meals were
served daily. Poor Sr. M. Agnes deserves a
rest after cooking for all these people
and the inconvenience of crossing the
lawn. But everybody seemed so resigned
and cheerful that you would be ashamed
to complain. Our crowning joy was the
appearance of our good Father Sullivan
on the scene; it seemed as though he fell
from Heaven to us; he has been such

LA CHARITE DE JESUS CRUCIFIE NOUS PRESSE

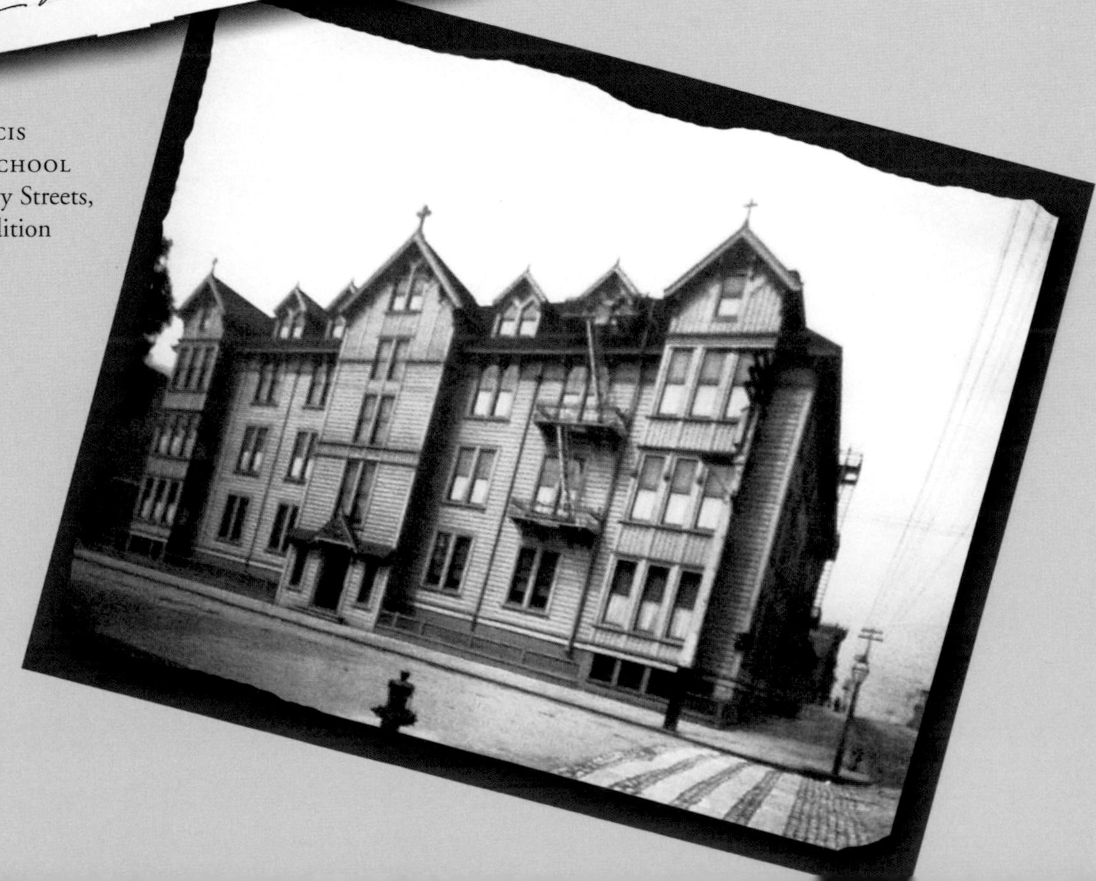

St. Francis Technical School
Gough and Geary Streets,
Western Addition

St. Francis Technical School
San Francisco, [California]
May 27, 1906

My dear Mother!

*T*he grace of Our Lord be with us forever!

It is only now that I feel I can write you at any length regarding the terrible ordeal through which we have passed. I shall never forget the morning of the 18th of April. I certainly thought that the last day had come for us all, and to make things worse I sprained my ankle Easter Monday; so there I was in bed in that little room off the hall when I was startled by the ringing of all the burglar alarms and such rocking and shaking of the building. I managed to get on our habit skirt and cornette and with the assistance of two of the large girls made my way to the Chapel. I saw that the Altar was intact; I then directed my attention to the children who were on their knees at their bedsides sending forth [ejaculatory prayers] and acts of contrition. In the meantime, we had the second shock which cracked the walls, threw down the chimneys, taking window, bricks and all through the roof. The statues are all broken, some entirely demolished. Thank God, there was not a child hurt, and all behaved so beautifully that it was such a comfort to us.

We were assembled on the lawn in fear and trembling. About eight o'clock we managed to get a cup of coffee on the gas stove, when we were frightened out by another slight shock. The next report was: the city was in flames and the water pipes were broken by the earthquake. We were sent by the Fire Department to collect what-ever valuables we had as they did not think they could control the fire. So, we had the children put on their best dresses and shoes and take a change of underwear and start out on a tramp to the [orphanages in South San Francisco]. A lady managed to get a carriage for me into which I succeeded in getting five or six of the delicate girls. We had all our valuable laces and trimmings bundled up ready to be sent out South.

It was a distressing sight to see the crowds of people fleeing to the Parks and Hills for safety. It was reported several times that the Technical and Cathedral were burned; but thank God both are standing, though badly shaken. The Friday follow-ing, our House was turned into a relief station and refuge for men, women and children. We had about one hundred fifty in the House; about five hundred meals were served daily. Poor Sister Mary Agnes deserves a rest after cooking for all these people and the inconvenience of cooking on the lawn; but everybody seemed so resigned and cheerful that you would be ashamed to complain.

Our crowning joy was the appearance of our good Father Sullivan on the scene; it seemed as though he fell from Heaven to us. He has been such a comfort to us all. He left us yesterday for Los Angeles. We have resumed work again and it is wonderful how busy we are kept, though we can hardly expect the work to be what it was as so many have lost their income and others have left the city. Father will be able to give you a full account of all. Miss B told me about your kindness to them and said that their dear old Mother cried with gratitude.

Father will tell you about our wanting to lease our house and grounds and go and live in Mr. F. J. Sullivan's old homestead, corner of Oak and Webster Streets. "The Madams" have leased theirs and now the Holy Family's House is for lease. Large buildings are in such demand.

Now, dear Mother, I have tried to give you some idea of what we have gone through; but I cannot do justice to the subject, so will have to leave the rest to our good Father to relate.

With love to you from each Sister, I am in the love of our Immaculate Mother,

Your devoted Child,

Sister Louise McCarron, [U.D.O.C.S.O.t.P.S. On Mission at St. Francis Technical School, Western Addition]

Sisters' Hospital
Los Angeles, [California]
June 22, 1906

Dear Mother!

*T*he grace of Our Lord be with us forever!

Our good Father Sullivan gave Sister Mary Agnes and me permission to spend a few weeks down here. Sister was all tired out after cooking for the poor people, and I felt if I could only get a few days away from the city, it would be a great help to me. The second Retreat opens this evening, so Father said I might remain for that. The Sisters have all been so good and kind to us that we are feeling so much better. I just put Sister Mary Agnes on the train for Santa Barbara where she will remain until after my Retreat. Father is beginning to look rested after his two Retreats. I cannot tell you what a comfort his visit was to his poor San Francisco children; it was like a ray of sunshine.

I have forgotten whether I told you we were trying to lease our House in my last letter. On the supposition that our work would not be sufficient to support, I thought of leasing our property as it is very valuable just at present, and going a little farther out where we could [rent] cheap. So, I just learned that it is leased for three years at one thousand per month to Ex-Mayor Phelan for the Relief Association. Mr. F. J. Sullivan, his brother-in-law, has given us their old home, corner of Webster and Oak, for two hundred per month. It will require some addition to accommodate all the children, but it will pay us to make [it] and the place will be very comfortable and convenient and we can have it at that price as long as we want. The parties taking our place are going to put up a five thousand dollar building on our vacant lot, which will revert to us at the end of the lease. I have asked Mr. Devlin for figures on our addition, and as soon as I hear, will let you know. We are not asked to make any repairs on our building at present. You know the walls are badly damaged from the earthquake.

Now, dear Mother, it is almost supper time. Pray for your poor children. Love from all.

Your devoted child,

Sister Louise McCarron, [U.D.O.C.S.O.t.P.S.
On Mission at St. Francis Technical
School, Western Addition]

Please excuse [the tear in this stationery paper].

1443 BRODERICK
STREET

1443 Broderick Street
San Francisco, Cal.
July 4, 1906.

We have a large sewing
school, where the children receive
abundance of material to work
up into dresses, aprons etc. for
themselves as other members of their
families.

We also visit the people in
their tents, bring them different
little pious articles. How eager
they are to get a prayer book,
"pair of beads" or a pair of
scapulars! They are even more
pious since the earthquake
as they still fear another, so
you can imagine how they
cling to any pious souvenir.

Mother Margaret,

My very dear Mother,

*T*he grace of Our Lord be forever with us!

Although I have never heard whether or not my two letters ever reached you, I feel that I must write again to let you know how we are getting along. First of all, are you feeling real well, dearest Mother? At times I fear that you are ill; otherwise you would have written to your daughters who have undergone great sufferings.

According to the advice of our dear Father Sullivan, six of us are located here until our new temporary school will be finished, which will be in about four weeks. A good Spanish lady and very kind friend offered us her house. She even went and procured permission from Father Sullivan before she offered it to us. Everything is most convenient and a little place of our own is immensely appreciated by us poor refugees. As to the future outlook of St. Vincent's School, I can say nothing. All we can do is to do the best we can, and I believe that God will bless our efforts to reestablish a school in which so much good was done. Our Pastor seems very hopeful.

Many thousands of people have gone forever from our poor city. Hundreds and hundreds have lost their minds and are now in the various insane asylums. Hundreds, yes thousands have been killed. So, you can imagine what a sad place San Francisco must be. Yet, there are thousands of children to be gathered in and instructed and their parents to be visited and comforted. This is the time for stout hearts and great work in San Francisco. We will have accommodations for four hundred pupils, and judging from their loyalty in the past, I feel that we will have a large attendance.

Everything is confusion yet. People are in tents on the outskirts of the city. Some are only awaiting their insurance in order to rebuild on old sites. Our Pastor thinks that if our school is reopened, the people will return to the Parish. Indeed, nobody can say how things will turn out. Everything looks dark. Still, I believe good will come from it all. God grant! I know that we must suffer much for the next two or three years trying to get St. Vincent's School again on its feet; but I would rather labor on in the very midst of the debris (as we will be located there) to bring our dear school into life again than to go to the finest Mission in the Community. When everything is going on well, then I care not how soon I leave it; but I would be almost heartbroken to be obliged to leave it as it now is. In our new temporary school, we will have everything very poor and I long for the plain walls and floors. My one desire is to adorn the young souls with all the beauty possible.

Yesterday, I saw the Vessel, Mongolia, pass through the "Golden Gate," bearing to us our beloved Father Lennon and three missionaries. Imagine our joy on seeing once more our dear, dear Father! He looks thin, but very bright and happy to meet us again. We are looking for a visit from Father Lennon and Father Sullivan today sometime. Our dear Father Sullivan looks real well and we are very sorry that his visitation is over and that we are about to lose him. He has been a dear kind Father to us in our great affliction. God bless and reward him!

My health at present is very good, though I was quite ill for two weeks. All of our Sisters are well and are very anxious to be in our own St. Vincent's once more. We have a large sewing school where the children receive abundance of material to work up into dresses, aprons, etc., for themselves and other members of their families. We also visit the people in their tents and bring them different little pious articles. How eager they are to get a prayer book, "pair of beads" or a pair of scapulars! They are even more pious since the earthquake and they still fear another, so you can imagine how they cling to any pious souvenir.

All of our little family, Sisters Mary Alice, Alexis, Estelle, Hyacinth and Caroline, join me in fondest love to you, our dear Mother.

In our Lord and St. Vincent,
your devoted daughter,

Sister Eugenia Garvey, U.D.o.C.S.o.t.P.S.
[On Mission at St. Vincent's School,
South of Market]

THE TEMPORARY CITY.

Miraculous Rehabilitation in Modest Homes of San Francisco's Trade and Commerce.

Mushroom Growth Recalls the Early Days of Metropolitan Development---Encouraging Outlook.

SAN FRANCISCO MONITOR
June 30, 1906

Many thousands of people have gone forever from our poor city. Hundreds and hundreds have lost their minds and are now in the various insane asylums. Hundreds, yes thousands have been killed. So, you can imagine what a sad place San Francisco must be.

—Sister Eugenia Garvey

In the book *Denial of Disaster,* Gladys Hansen reports that after the earthquake and fire, there were refugees who committed suicide or were judged insane and committed to mental hospitals.

SOURCE: *Denial of Disaster* by Gladys Hansen and others; published by Cameron and Company, San Francisco, 1989; page 126.

talking a great deal of the
newer San Francisco If you
could go over the city dear
sister, and see the ruin and
desolation as far as the eye
can reach. And ride all
day in an electric car for
miles and miles and see
nothing but debris. Even the
streets are packed with bricks,
tangled wires, twisted iron
pipes, etc. Then the property
on Market street that was
considered so valuable, signs
up on every side for leases
God help the poor this
coming winter. There will be
terrible sufferings among them
when the rainy season
come on. They are living
in tents all over the city
It is almost impossible for

LA CHARITE DE JESUS CRUCIFIE NOUS PRESSE

Mount St. Joseph's
N Street and 19th Avenue, Silver Terrace

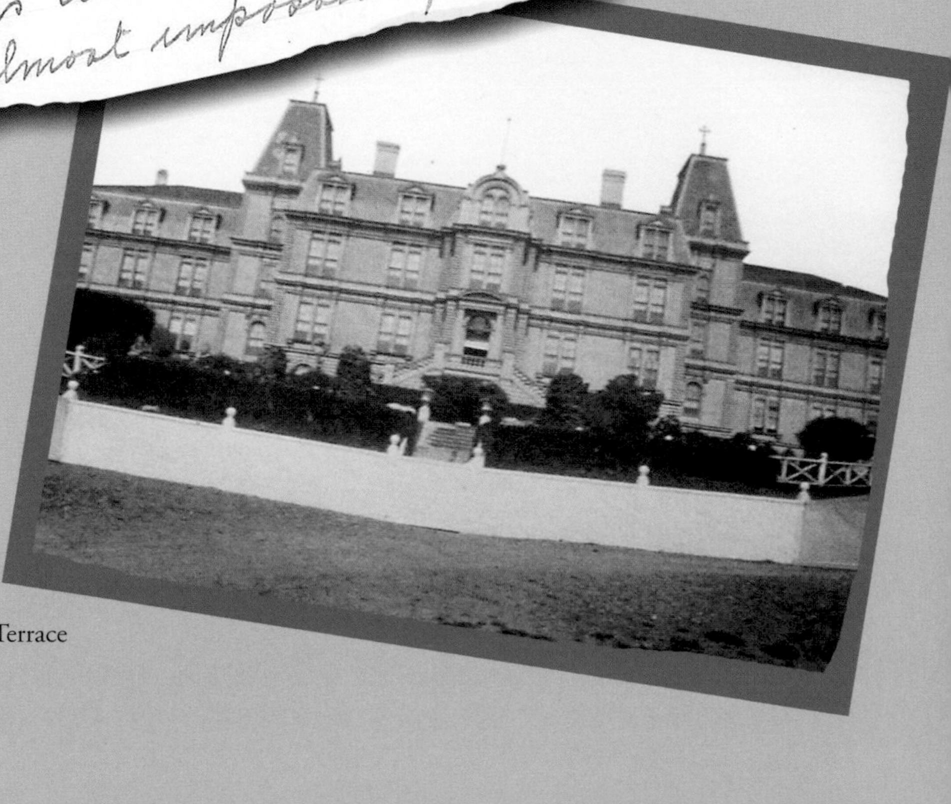

San Francisco, California
July 17, 1906

My dear Sister,

*T*he grace of Our Lord be with us forever!

I am sending you a booklet of the ruined Catholic Churches, also the San Francisco Magazine. It began in May. They were taken up so quickly, it was difficult to get one. But the second edition is out for May. They will send it to you from the Agent. . . . There is no June number. The last of this month, the July number will be out and will continue on for the year. It is well written up and will treat principally of the San Francisco calamity. If it lightens your labor and helps you in any way, dear Sister, I shall feel well repaid.

Thank God, our dear Sister Stanislaus R. is a little better. She has been a great sufferer since April. Last week, we were able to give her a change of air and scene. We took her in a chair to the fire escape. The little tots saw her going and they gathered from all directions. They held a little reception all to themselves and told how much they prayed for her. One little one said, "Sister, I pray much for you; I say, 'Out of the depths,'" which gave Sister a hearty laugh.

The big men here are talking a great deal of the newer San Francisco. If you could go over the city, dear Sister, and see the ruins and desolation as far as the eye can reach, and ride all day in an electric car for miles and miles, [you would] see nothing but debris. Even the streets are packed with bricks, tangled wires, twisted iron pipes, etc. Then the property on Market Street that was considered so valuable has signs up on every side for leases.

God help the poor this coming winter. There will be terrible sufferings among them when the rainy season comes on. They are living in tents all over the city. It is almost impossible for a woman to get employment. And they have now begun to charge them rent for the tents.

Sister Stanislaus R. is going to send you a little statue of our Blessed Mother. It went through the earthquake and fire. Mr. Frank Sullivan brought it out from his house to Sister. Four of our brothers are attending the University in Berkeley. They come on Friday P.M. and stay with us until Sunday P.M. They are going to give us a Solemn High Mass on our Holy Founder's Day. About the ferns, dear Sister, I am afraid they would be no use to you after going by mail. Better wait an opportunity of somebody taking them. You shall not be cheated out of them.

Much love to our dear Mother and all in the Valley with a large share to your own dear self. Say a little prayer for your unworthy,

Sister Martina [Moran], U.D.o.C.S.o.t.P.S.
[On Mission at Mount St. Joseph's,
Silver Terrace]

If you could go over the city, dear Sister,
and see the ruins and desolation as far
as the eye can reach, and ride all day
in an electric car for miles and miles, you
would see nothing but debris. Even the
streets are packed with bricks, tangled
wires, twisted iron pipes, etc.

—SISTER MARTINA MORAN

In the book *Denial of Disaster,* there are numerous photographs that depict San Francisco in ruins with collapsed buildings, streets filled with rubble, etc. Gladys Hansen indicates that many San Franciscans did not clear rubble from their property until insurance claims were settled.

SOURCE: *Denial of Disaster* by Gladys Hansen and others; published by Cameron and Company, San Francisco, 1989; page 149.

St. Vincent's
Temporary School
Fifth and Clementina Streets,
South of Market

The whole city is interested in those who have pluck enough to rebuild in "burnt district"; they all will be surprised in a few months to see our school an garden a veritable oasis in the great desert.

We have suffered considerably — but cheerfully and resignedly, any now we start again to instruct the children

St. Vincent's
1443 Broderick Street
San Francisco, California
July 23, 1906

My very dear Mother Margaret,

*T*he grace of Our Lord be forever with us!

I trust, dear Mother, that you are feeling well after your Retreat and that the warm weather may not be too trying upon you.

Our dear Father Sullivan has, doubtlessly, told you everything about us; for he was so long with us [that] he knows just how we are situated. He was, indeed, a loving Father to us in our day of trial. Nobody on earth could be kinder. How highly favored we were to have our dear Father Sullivan and Father Lennon both with us for a time!

On St. Vincent's Day, dear Father Lennon came up to our city. He came directly to us and dined here. His presence here made us very happy. He looked well and seemed very bright and happy.

You will be pleased to know that our new school is progressing rapidly and that we will reopen on the 6th of August. God willing! The pupils are very loyal to their school and although scattered about, they are to return to St. Vincent's. Owing to the fact that twenty-nine public schools and six neighboring parochial schools are not to reopen, we are convinced that a large number of pupils will present themselves for admission into our well-equipped temporary school.

Our dear Father Sullivan promised our Pastor, Father Rogers, that if the number of pupils necessitated the return of our teachers, we would get them back. Without calling for registration, two hundred have presented themselves. We must have our grades preserved; therefore, we will need at least three more Sisters. We will have more large pupils than small, owing to the distance they must come. The high school pupils are all coming back; hence, a teacher is necessary. Sister F, now with the little children in Boyle Heights, taught this class. She is not the teacher that such a class requires; but if no better can be sent, we would be satisfied to get her back. She is a good little Sister, but not a remarkably good teacher. Sister W of Hollister would be far more capable in such a class. I feel sure that Sister W's family would not bother her were she here (I know you will forgive me).

Our Commercial High School is absolutely necessary to the success of the school and to the support of the Community here; by it we get employment for many of our pupils. This Department has a good reputation in our city. Businessmen accept, without hesitation, the graduates of St. Vincent's Commercial High

School. Every graduate holds a fine position in good firms. I have never accepted for these young ladies a position in doctors' or lawyers' offices. They are all engaged in large business firms where many young women are engaged. Businessmen have congratulated us on the sterling qualities of our graduates. Sister Caroline Collins has charge of this High School.

The eighth-year classes are very important. Sister Alexis has the boys and we have no good teacher for the eighth grade of girls. Sister L used to teach it. Dear Mother, there are good teachers in other duties who could do so much in schools. Sister P, now out at [Mount St. Joseph's], could teach the girls' grade well. We expect both Sister Z and Sister N back. We need them for seventh and sixth grades of boys and girls. Both are capable of teaching these grades, but I do think that Sister Z should not be with Sister N; they are better apart. Still, if you send them to us, I am satisfied.

It would be the greatest help to our struggling institution, just arising from her ashes, if you could send us a good music teacher. Music must go far towards supporting our House for the next two years. The majority of pupils can pay nothing, but pupils from suburban districts will continue to take music. Many convents in which music was taught are no longer in existence.

We have lots to do; may God's blessings help us through. Our school will, God willing, open August 6; but we cannot live in our apartments for two or three weeks later, as carpenters are trying to finish the children's portion of the building in order to gather them in as soon as possible (Public Schools opened last Monday). Our apartments will be plastered and finished neatly. The school is very large, classrooms 18 x 32. We are trying to get free books for pupils who resided in burnt district.

Our sewing classes are large and doing excellent work. Red Cross Society is now very kind to us. We are furnished with all the goods we can use in Sewing Class. Five sewing machines were sent to us by the Relief Committee. Even after school resumes, we will have pupils continue to sew.

The whole city is interested in those who have pluck enough to rebuild in "burnt district." They all will be surprised in a few months to see our school and garden, a veritable oasis in the great desert. We have suffered considerably, but cheerfully and resignedly; and now we start again to instruct the children, to cultivate our desolate corner of the Master's Vineyard; and I firmly hope that He is with us. We have nothing but Him; we desire but Him.

You, dear Mother, will I know promptly send us three good teachers and perhaps a music teacher: Sister F, Boyle Heights, and Sister N, now in Technical School, simply walking about the sewing class keeping order, not teaching at all (many Sisters could keep order, having no teaching to do). Sister N is a good sixth-year teacher. Sister Z teaches the seventh grade; she is doing very little [at Mount St. Joseph Infant Asylum]. If she could replace Sister P at [Mount St. Joseph's], to give suggestions, it might work better for Sister N and Sister Z. . . . Father Rogers wants Sisters F, N and Z back, for he says the pupils want their old teachers and they ought to have them. I beg of you, dear Mother, to have three good teachers, and I hope good Sisters, here in time to begin class work on the 9th of August. Nine Sisters will be very different from seventeen. I hope our number will grow. How happy I would be to receive Sister L and Sister K back again.

. . . I am with fondest love in the Sacred Heart of our Lord,

Yours devotedly,

Sister Eugenia Garvey, U.D.O.C.S.O.T.P.S.
[On Mission at St. Vincent's School,
South of Market]

FATHER JOHN SULLIVAN, C.M.

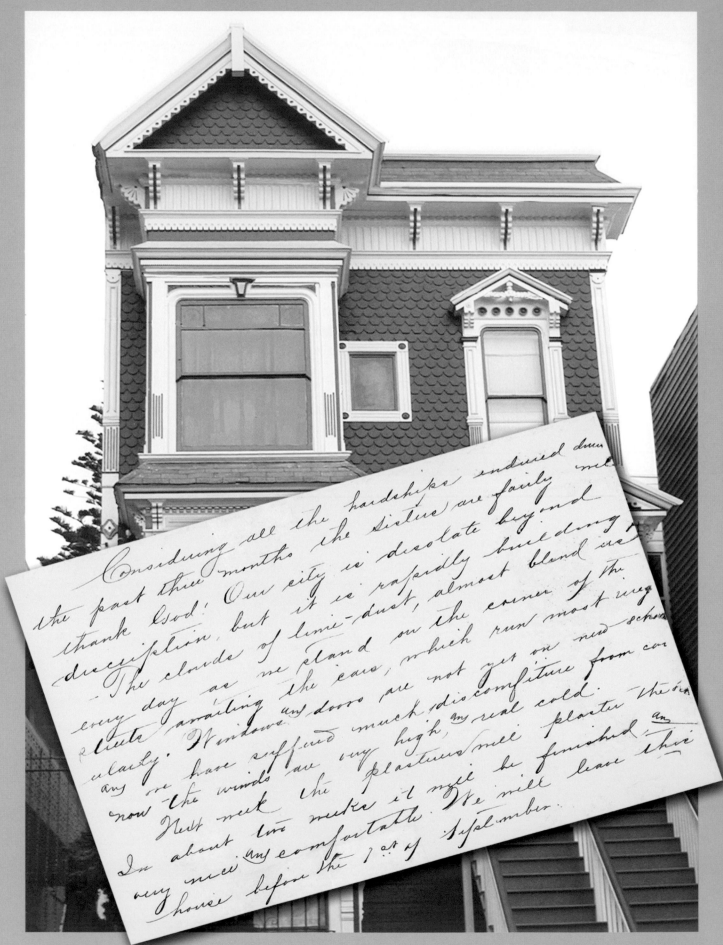

Considering all the hardships endured during the past three months the Sisters are fairly well thank God! Our city is desolate beyond description, but it is rapidly building up. The clouds of lime-dust, almost blind us every day as we stand on the corner awaiting the cars, which run most irregularly. Windows and doors are not yet in, now the winds are very high, and real cold.

Next week the plasterers will plaster the house. In about two weeks it will be finished and very nice and comfortable. We will leave this house before the 1st of September.

1443 BRODERICK STREET

Mother Margaret,

My very dear Mother,

*T*he grace of Our Lord be forever with us!

I trust that this letter may find you real well and rested after the heavy work of Retreat communications, etc. We have been teaching for the past three weeks in our unfinished school; over three hundred and fifty boys and girls crowd the classrooms. Many are awaiting the completion of the building. I believe we will have over four hundred in a few weeks. Up to the present, we have taught under great difficulties; but in a few weeks the school will be comfortable.

Our High School has no teacher. Twenty-five large pupils await their teacher. It is hard to break up a course of study half entered upon. Sister F taught this class; I beg of you, dear Mother, to send her or an equally competent teacher to take this class as soon as possible. It is from the High School Department we get pupils for the Commercial Department, and it is upon this we greatly depend for our support. We need a music teacher very, very badly, for to these resources we look for the principal means of support.

Dear Mother Margaret, we have sufferings enough in poor San Francisco at present without having to worry over a big class of pupils without a teacher. Everything seems against us; but I beg of you for God's sake to send us two teachers, good teachers, one for the high school and one for the sixth grade. Then, if you send us a music teacher, we will get along very nicely. Sister Z has not started to teach. She has a severe cold. She will teach over fifty seventh-year pupils. . . .

Considering all the hardships endured during the past three months, the Sisters are fairly well, thank God! Our city is desolate beyond description, but it is rapidly building [up]. The clouds of lime dust almost blind us everyday as we stand on the corner of the streets awaiting the cars which run most irregularly. Windows and doors are not yet on our new school, and we have suffered much discomfiture from the cold; now the winds are very high and real cold. Next week the plasterers will plaster the school. In about two weeks it will be finished and very nice and comfortable. We will leave this house before the 1st of September.

A beautiful letter from Our Most Honored Mother, Marie Kieffer, reached me last week. She appears so interested in our poor little Mission and its future success. Well, God knows what is in store for us! I trust that our little school may live on and sow good seed in the hearts of many.

Whilst the world turns a pitying eye upon our poor city, I feel sure that our Mother's charity will send us two good teachers to help build up the scattered parish by drawing and teaching well hundreds of children. I am not anxious to remain here, naturally I long to leave it; but obedience holds me here and, therefore, I believe that by His grace I may do some little good. But Mother dearest, please come to my aid. Send me two good teachers to take the large classes now awaiting them! Will you not have pity on my poor nerves, already wracked and tortured by sufferings worthy of the name? Give me a start in the new school. Give it a chance to succeed and then if it fails, we can do no more.

All the Sisters join me in sincere love to you, our dear Mother. Daily I pray for you. May God protect you!

Yours in our Lord and St. Vincent,
Most devotedly,

Sister Eugenia Garvey, U.D.O.C.S.O.T.P.S.
[On Mission at St. Vincent's School,
South of Market]

*The combined St. Vincent's School
and St. Patrick's Boys' School was now known
as St. Vincent's Temporary School.*

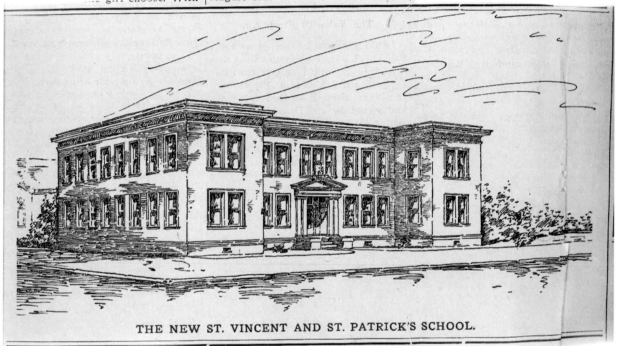

St. Vincent's and St. Patrick's Schools

St. Vincent's and St. Patrick's Schools, conducted by the Sisters of Charity, will reopen at the corner of Fifth and Clementina streets about August 6th.

THE NEW ST. VINCENT AND ST. PATRICK'S SCHOOL.

A large, commodious, well-equipped building has been erected which will accommodate hundreds of boys and girls.

The High School embraces the regular academic branches, commercial, gives thorough training in shorthand, typewriting, bookkeeping, commercial correspondence, Spanish, etc.

SAN FRANCISCO MONITOR
July 21, 1906

Hollister

Notes

written by the
Sisters from the Mission
in Hollister

HOLLISTER, April 28.—The schools of Hollister were all closed without warning by the earthquake. The Grammar School tried to reopen last Monday, but only 80 pupils met, so after some consideration, it was decided to postpone school until April 30. The Grammar School stood the shake very well, only two of the rooms and the assembly hall having the plaster knocked off. The County High School will also reopen Monday. The school of the Sacred Heart reopened last Monday, and as their school building was completely wrecked the sisters are at present occupying one of the Berberich cottages on Sixth street.

SUNDAY MERCURY AND HERALD
San Jose, California, Sunday Morning, April 29, 1906

Sacred Heart School, Hollister.

The School of the Sacred Heart at Holister was so badly damaged that it will have to be rebuilt. A movement is now on foot to raise funds for its reconstruction. While the movement has not as yet taken definite shape those having the matter in charge have met with so much encouragement that there appears to be no doubt but that the necessary funds will be raised. The people of Hollister, always liberal, will be particularly so when called upon to help the noble sisters take up again their life work.

SAN FRANCISCO MONITOR
May 19, 1906

[The Sisters at Sacred Heart School in Hollister wrote about their recovery from the earthquake. These Notes were written around 1907, or later.]

*O*ur House was destroyed by Earthquake on April 18, 1906; there were six Sisters with Sister Teresa as Sister Servant [Sister who was in charge]. The School was kept [open in a] Cottage for one month. The Sisters lived in the Crepin House until June 2. Father Sullivan came to Hollister. He returned to San Francisco where he [gave] the Retreat; Sisters Mary Angela and Teresa went up to make it.

After the Retreat, Sister Teresa came back to Hollister and met with the Bishop (Conaty). Four Sisters, Josephine, Camilla, Bernadette, Vincent, and five children left Saturday, June 2. The children went to spend vacation in Santa Cruz and the Sisters [went to Los Angeles] to make the Retreat given by Father Sullivan. Sisters Mary Angela and Teresa moved back to our own grounds and lived in the washhouse. Mrs. P. Sullivan gave us her old stove. The School closed on May 22, 1906.

We opened the School on August 21 in tents and had a splendid attendance. We taught there until November when the classroom in the House was ready for us. The children (boarders) slept and ate in the laundry. Sisters slept in the little room in the yard and ate in the [trunk] house. We remained here until Christmas Eve, when we had our supper in the refectory in the House; the children ate in the kitchen. Such a winter [we have had with] storms, rain, snow, etc., etc. Three of the umbrella trees in the front yard were blown [down] one day, a dreadful wind storm. April 28, Holy Thursday, the Chapel was not quite ready, but on Friday [Father] said Mass and left our dear Lord with us. Early Saturday, just as the last bench was moved into the Chapel, we had a very heavy earthquake; thank God, no damage was done.

SACRED HEART SCHOOL
Sixth and West Streets, Hollister

San Francisco

Memoirs

of the 1906 Earthquake and Fire
shared in later years
by Sister Alexis Kuhn

St. Vincent's Temporary School
Fifth and Clementina Streets, South of Market

Sister Alexis Kuhn

Steel Frame

On April 18, St. Vincent's School on Mission and Third and St. Patrick's Boys' School on Natoma and Fourth were both demolished by the earthquake and fire that devastated the area South of Market. Six Sisters remained in San Francisco to help rebuild their two schools amid the ruins and debris; they were called the Steel Frame. In early August, a combined St. Vincent's Temporary School opened on the corner of Fifth and Clementina.

ACCOUNT OF THE EARTHQUAKE AND FIRE AS TOLD BY SISTER ALEXIS KUHN (CONTINUED):

Life went on in the shattered city much as life goes on anytime, anywhere. Former parishioners did not return to St. Patrick's Parish, but looked for possible future residential areas in which to build their homes. San Francisco charged with the vigor of youth turned to the task of rebuilding. The new [School's] two-story frame building was erected at Fifth and Clementina Streets and ready for occupancy in September, but beset with a flood of overwhelming difficulties in every direction. Registration first week reached one hundred and thirty pupils, all of whom had been at the old Schools, but now commuters, living not nearer than a ten-mile radius of approach to the School. . . .

APRIL 18, 1906 (CONTINUED):

Mrs. Mahoney, a benefactor, placed her home on Broderick Street in Holy Cross Parish at our disposal. We remained here until September when we again returned to St. Patrick's Parish, where we started school under great difficulties with an attendance of nearly two hundred pupils. During our stay at Broderick Street we spent the time in the interests of our people regarding housing, occupation, and material benefits necessary for subsistence and support.

REBUILDING A CITY.

The Gigantic Task which San Francisco has Tackled with Boundless Faith and Courage.

Some of the Physical Difficulties that Preclude Miraculous Expedition in the Work of Reconstruction.

SAN FRANCISCO MONITOR
October 6, 1906

San Francisco

From the **Biography**
of Sister Caroline Collins
written in 1952 by
Sister Vincentine Lancaster

*Fires started in different directions:
behind us, on the sides and on the corners,
and no water could be had, for the
earthquake had wrenched the pipes.*

—Sister Mary Alice Maginnis

*We were out before seven o'clock, running
from the fire....We started down Mission
Street from Second and could not get to
Third by any means. No wagons were to be
had and we just escaped with our lives.*

—Sister Mary Alice Maginnis

Steel Frame

SISTER EUGENIA
GARVEY

SISTER CAROLINE
COLLINS

"Six remained. Neither the earthquake nor the fire could daunt them. They were called the 'steel frame.' The name derived from the fact that when the destruction and havoc had all been wrecked, there stood forth in the bare city only the twisted steel frames of buildings. They were an invitation to an heroic people to come and build a bigger and a better San Francisco.

"This the people did.

"The six Sisters: Sister Eugenia, Sister Mary Alice, Sister Caroline, Sister Alexis, Sister Estelle and Sister Hyacinth were the steel frame for a new school which would soon be a building.

"Temporarily their days were devoted to helping the Red Cross take care of the sick and wounded. Abandoned car barns on the outskirts of the city were used as Red Cross headquarters. They welcomed all the help they could get.

"A week or so later a Mrs. Mahoney, who lived on Broderick Street, offered her home to the Sisters so that they would not have to travel so many miles back and forth everyday. Although she found other lodgings for herself, she left her housekeeper to cook for and to take care of the six Sisters.

"It was there that Sister Caroline became the leader in trying to locate the former pupils of the school. She thought they should lose as little time as possible and had already obtained Mrs. Mahoney's consent to use her home for a temporary school. . . ."

From: *Faith Aflame* by Sister Vincentine Lancaster, D.C.

SISTER ESTELLE
MURPHY

SISTER ALEXIS
KUHN

SISTER HYACINTH
MCNEAL

SISTER MARY
ALICE MAGINNIS

St. Vincent's Temporary School
Fifth and Clementina Streets, South of Market

St. Vincent's Pupils

Pupils and Their Families

*T*he Sisters knew that many of the families of their pupils were refugees living in the camps and warehouses set up around the city. They went in search of these families to gather the children for school and to comfort their parents. Some of the pupils returned to the new temporary school located at Fifth and Clementina, other pupils and their families moved away from the area.

Sister Margaret Mary Dillon, a contemporary Daughter of Charity, remembers the stories of her parents who were among those former pupils who became refugees living in the camps and warehouses around the city. Both of her parents were among those former pupils whose families eventually moved back to the area South of Market after the earthquake and fire.

Sister Margaret Mary Dillon, D.C.
Our Lady of the Visitacion School,
San Francisco

The Daughters of Charity felt the special pro-
tection of Divine Providence during
the days of the earthquake and fire.
Although their buildings were demolished
and badly damaged, there was
no loss of life and no serious injuries to
those under their care or to the
Sisters themselves. Thanks be to God!

Note of Gratitude

The Daughters of Charity suffered no loss of life and no serious injuries among those under their care or among the Sisters themselves during the devastating earthquake and fire. At the time, the Sisters had nine Missions in San Francisco and the nearby cities. Early records and documents yield enough information that the number of children, patients, elderly and Sisters on each of these Missions at the time of the earthquake can be approximated.

Four of the Missions were demolished: St. Vincent's School and St. Patrick's Boys' School (day schools) had no children on the premises due to the early hour, but about twenty Sisters were in residence there; Mary's Help Hospital had no patients and no Sisters on the premises, as it was not yet in operation; Sacred Heart School had day scholars who were not on the premises due to the early hour, but eleven children (boarders) and six Sisters were in residence there.

Two Missions were severely damaged: St. Francis Technical School, with ninety children and about eight Sisters in residence; and O'Connor Sanitarium, with about forty patients and elderly and about thirteen Sisters in residence.

Three Missions were slightly damaged: Mount St. Joseph's and Mount St. Joseph Infant Asylum, with about 700 children and about thirty-two Sisters in residence; Holy Cross School had day scholars who were not on the premises due to the early hour, but 145 children and about ten Sisters were in residence there.

That no lives were lost and no serious injuries occurred was an act of Divine Providence, and of this the Sisters were conscious and expressive in their letters. As Sister Mary Joseph wrote in her letter, "We can feel the immense goodness of God and the truth of what St. Vincent says, 'Our Lord watches over the Daughters of Charity with a most special care.'"

*The San Francisco Earthquake and Fire of 1906
was devastating. Hundreds of thousands were
homeless. Thousands were dead and thousands injured.
Hundreds of city blocks and tens of thousands
of buildings were destroyed. Many thousands
of dwellings were demolished.*

Some Basic Facts

The San Francisco Earthquake and Fire of 1906 was devastating. There were deaths, injuries, loss of property, and no means of communication or transportation within the city. Here are some basic facts gathered almost a century later:

- At least 3,000 were dead and thousands were injured.

- Almost 200,000 were homeless. This was almost one half of the population of San Francisco. Many remained in the city, while others fled.

- Much of the city was burned (from the Bay to Van Ness Avenue).

- Nearly 500 city blocks were destroyed.

- Tens of thousands of buildings were destroyed (most of which were dwellings).

- Communication and transportation, as well as business and financial dealings, were all disrupted.

SOURCES:

Denial of Disaster by Gladys Hansen and others; published by Cameron and Company, San Francisco, 1989.

The Virtual Museum of the City of San Francisco Web site: www.sfmuseum.org

Chapter Four

Through the Years
1906 ~ 2006

Nine Missions

A Postscript

Through the years, the Works of the Daughters
of Charity have continued in
San Francisco and the nearby cities.
The Sisters lived through the earthquake
and other tragedies, but they recovered,
and their Works survived and continue to
the present day.

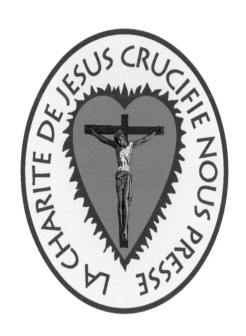

Through the Years

Although Mount St. Joseph's and Mount St. Joseph Infant Asylum escaped the earthquake and fire in 1906 with little or no damage, tragedy struck in 1910. In the early hours of October 9, a fire broke out and consumed the building that housed Mount St. Joseph's. Two years later, it moved into a new building constructed on the same site as the old one. Mount St. Joseph's continued for many decades in this building in the Silver Terrace area (later known as Bay View and Newhall Streets). Today, this original orphanage begun in 1852 continues as Mount St. Joseph – St. Elizabeth located on Masonic Avenue. Mount St. Joseph Infant Asylum, undamaged by the 1906 Earthquake and Fire or by the 1910 fire, continued at its Silver Terrace location until it was discontinued in 1914.

St. Francis Technical School (trade school) was discontinued in 1928, and eventually its building became available. St. Vincent's Grade and High Schools continued in their "temporary school" at Fifth and Clementina Streets until the High School moved into this available building on Gough and Geary Streets. Today, this original school begun in 1852 continues as Sacred Heart Cathedral Preparatory located on Ellis Street. The Grade School continued at Fifth and Clementina Streets for many years (renamed St. Patrick's Parish School).

O'Connor Sanitarium, renamed O'Connor Hospital, eventually moved to a new location on Forest Avenue where it continues today. Likewise, Mary's Help Hospital eventually moved from San Francisco to Daly City and was later renamed Seton Medical Center; it continues at this location today.

The Sisters withdrew from both Sacred Heart School and Holy Cross School many decades ago; however, the schools continue today. Sacred Heart School is located on College Street in Hollister, and Holy Cross School on Emmet Street in Santa Cruz.

Link with the Past

Sister Alexis Kuhn had come to San Francisco in 1887 and taught at St. Patrick's Boys' School until the earthquake and fire of 1906. After living through the tragedy of April 18, she remained to help with the wounded and then to locate and comfort the people of their parish who were also refugees. She was one of six Sisters who stayed in San Francisco to regroup and help rebuild a school for their pupils. These six Sisters referred to themselves as the "steel frame"; they opened a combined temporary school in early August, less than four months after the earthquake and fire. Sister Alexis taught the boys' classes here until 1921 when she left her beloved St. Vincent's School, yet she maintained contact through the years with many of her former pupils. She died in 1972 at the age of 102.

After St. Patrick's Parish School on Fifth and Clementina closed, a low-cost housing project for the elderly was erected on this same site. It was named Alexis Apartments in memory of Sister Alexis and her thirty-four years of continuing service in San Francisco.

SISTER ALEXIS KUHN
ON HER 100TH BIRTHDAY

MOUNT ST. JOSEPH–ST. ELIZABETH
100 Masonic Avenue, San Francisco

SETON MEDICAL CENTER
1900 Sullivan Avenue, Daly City

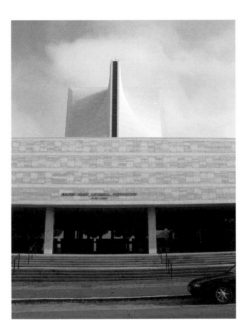

SACRED HEART CATHEDRAL
PREPARATORY
1055 Ellis Street, San Francisco

O'CONNOR HOSPITAL
2105 Forest Avenue, San Jose

Acknowledgements

WE ARE INDEBTED TO THESE ELEVEN SISTERS WHOSE
WRITINGS MADE POSSIBLE THIS COMMEMORATIVE BOOK:

————

SISTER MARY JOSEPH O'LEARY

SISTER VINCENTIA HALLIGAN

SISTER LOUISE MCCARRON

SISTER MARY ALICE MAGINNIS

SISTER EUGENIA GARVEY

SISTER GENEVIEVE JOHNSON

SISTER VICTORINE FITZGERALD

SISTER TERESA HILL

SISTER HELENA MCGHAN

SISTER MARTINA MORAN

SISTER ALEXIS KUHN

Acknowledgements

CREDITS (GRAPHICS)

Courtesy, Archives Daughters of
Charity, Emmitsburg, Maryland:
Page 15, photos (upper right,
upper left, lower right)
Page 16, photos (two)
Page 17, photos (three)
Page 27, photo
Page 32, photo
Page 36, photo
Page 52, photo (upper left)
Page 56, photo (upper left)
Page 62, photo
Page 75, photo
Page 82, photo
Page 83, photo
Page 100, photo
Page 108, photo
Page 123, photo

Courtesy, Archives of the
Archdiocese of San Francisco:
Cover, photo
Page 2, photo
Page 6, photo (center)
Page 19, photo
Page 23, photos (three)
Page 48, newspaper
Page 86, photo (lower right)
Page 98, newspaper
Page 106, newspaper
Page 112, newspaper
Page 119, newspaper
Page 122, newspaper (lower right)
Page 127, newspaper
Page 130, photo
Page 142, photo

Courtesy, San Francisco History
Center, San Francisco Public Library:
Page 11, photo
Page 14, map from *The California
Earthquake of 1906*
Page 22, map from *San Francisco
and Vicinity, Before and After the
Great Fire*
Page 26, photo
Page 28-29, photo
Page 41, photo
Page 42, photo (upper)
Page 49, photo
Page 50-51, photo
Page 50, newspaper (three)
Page 51, newspaper (two)
Page 55, newspaper
Page 59, photo
Page 80, photo (upper)
Page 87, photo
Page 107, photo
Page 111, photo

Courtesy, History San Jose:
Page 41, newspaper
Page 64, newspaper
Page 66, newspaper
Page 72, newspaper (two)
Page 74, newspaper
Page 77, newspaper
Page 87, newspaper (two)
Page 122, newspaper (lower left)

Courtesy, San Benito County
Historical Museum:
Page 70, photo
Page 76, photo

Courtesy, Sister Estela Morales, D.C.:
Page 104, photo
Page 116, photo
Page 133, photo
Page 139, photo
Page 143, photos (four)

Acknowledgements

CREDITS (TEXT)

Faith Aflame, Sister Vincentine Lancaster, 1952 (page 46):
Pages 2, 131, excerpts

Genesis of the Company, 1633–1968 (page 7):
Page 8, excerpt

Annals of the Congregation of the Mission or A Collection of Edifying Letters,
1906 (pages 455–456):
Pages 43, 130, letter

Courtesy of Cameron & Company; Gladys Hansen:
Pages 26, 42, 49, 59, 80, 107, 111, excerpts
Page 137, excerpts

Courtesy of the Virtual Museum of the City of San Francisco,
Gladys Hansen:
Page 99, excerpt
Page 137, excerpts

CREDITS (OTHER)

The California Earthquake of 1906, edited by David Starr Jordan (article
by Grove Karl Gilbert); published by A.M. Robertson, 1907 (page 217):
Page 14, map showing position of fault that caused the 1906 Earthquake

San Francisco and Vicinity, Before and After the Great Fire; published by
Rieder-Cardinell Company, 1906 (third page):
Page 22, map showing burned area from the 1906 Earthquake and Fire

Early Records / Documents: Admission Records from Mount St. Joseph –
St. Elizabeth; Annual Reports from the Archdiocese of San Francisco; U.S.
Census Records from 1900 and 1910.
Page 135

SELECTED BIBLIOGRAPHY

Burns, Jeffrey. *San Francisco, A History of the Archdiocese of San Francisco,*
Volume 2. Strasbourg: Editions du Signe.

Hansen, Gladys, and Emmet Condon. *Denial of Disaster.* San Francisco:
Cameron and Company, 1989.

Kurzman, Dan. *Disaster! The Great San Francisco Earthquake and Fire of*
1906. New York: Perennial, An Imprint of Harper Collins Publishers, 2002.

Lancaster, Sister Vincentine, D.C. *Faith Aflame: The Story of Sister Caroline*
Collins. St. Louis: Wellington, 1952.

Thomas, Gordon, and Max Morgan Witts. *The San Francisco Earthquake.*
New York: Stein and Day Publishers, 1971.

The Virtual Museum of the City of San Francisco Web site
(www.sfmuseum.org).

Archives of Seton Provincialate

All telegrams and letters written to Mother Margaret O'Keefe and other Daughters of Charity except letter credited on previous page.

All notes, memoirs and biographical excerpts.

All graphics of handwritten documents (telegrams, letters and notes).

All photographs, newspapers and excerpts not credited on previous pages.

All early records and documents not credited on previous pages.

Commemorative Book

Research/Writing/Editing:
Sister Margaret Ann Gainey (Daughters of Charity, Seton Provincialate, Los Altos Hills, California)

Illustrations/Graphics:
Sister Estela Morales (Daughters of Charity, Seton Provincialate, Los Altos Hills, California)

Design/Layout:
Sister Margaret Ann Gainey and Sister Estela Morales (Daughters of Charity, Seton Provincialate, Los Altos Hills, California)

Publishing and Printing Consultant:
Hinckle & Sons Printing Office, San Francisco; Año Nuevo Island Press

Graphic Design:
Marianne Hinckle, Año Nuevo Island Press

Legal Advisor:
Alan C. Freeland of Cooper, White & Cooper LLP

*Our gratitude
to the Daughters of Charity Foundation,
who made possible the
publication of this commemorative book
through a generous grant*

Our Gratitude

We, the Daughters of Charity, are grateful to all those who helped us in the preparation of this Commemorative Book, especially:

Alan C. Freeland, of Cooper, White & Cooper LLP, who counseled us on legal and publishing issues throughout our editorial review.

Gladys Hansen, San Francisco City Archivist Emeritus, who guided us during the preparation of our book; we are grateful for her years of research and authorship of *Denial of Disaster*.

Jeffrey Burns, Archivist of the Archdiocese of San Francisco, who made available earthquake photographs and newspaper articles (those wonderful old copies of the Monitor).

Susan Goldstein, City Archivist, and Richard Marino (San Francisco History Center, San Francisco Public Library), who helped us gather photographs and newspaper articles for our book; we are especially grateful for the Library's historical photograph collection online, as well as its 1906 newspaper collection.

Jim R. Reed, Archivist of History San Jose, who helped us gather newspaper articles for our book from a collection of original 1906 newspapers.

Earlene McCabe, Docent of the San Benito County Historical Museum, and Jack O'Donnell, Board Member of the San Benito County Historical Heritage Committee, who helped us gather photographs and shared local history.

Robert W. Cameron, Publisher of Cameron & Company, whose support and generosity towards us is appreciated; we are grateful for his publication of *Denial of Disaster*.

William J. Maher, Archivist of the University of Illinois, whose knowledge of legal issues related to archives has been a great help to us.

Dear Readers,

We, the Daughters of Charity, thank you for your interest in the "Steel Frames." Our Sisters' personal accounts of the 1906 earthquake are their gift to us in 2006. We wanted to share their inspiring story with you.

Gratefully,

Sister Margaret Keaveney, Visitatrix
Province of The West

Proceeds from sales of Steel Frames *will be used for our Daughters of Charity Missions at the service of the poor.*

...chosen pio...
...Western daughters; we...
...ving in our Chapel thi...
the children sang the...
all our hearts sang in...
little voices; we cha...
Sunday, so you see...
Dear Sr. Stanislausje,...
weak, she sits up frail...
Mass this morning. And...
...ers for us all, and...